The Bridge to Humanity

How Affect Hunger Trumps the Selfish Gene

Walter Goldschmidt

University of California, Los Angeles

New York   Oxford
OXFORD UNIVERSITY PRESS
2006

Oxford University Press, Inc., publishes works that further Oxford University's objective of excellence in research, scholarship, and education.

Oxford New York
Auckland   Cape Town   Dar es Salaam   Hong Kong   Karachi
Kuala Lumpur   Madrid   Melbourne   Mexico City   Nairobi
New Delhi   Shanghai   Taipei   Toronto

With offices in
Argentina   Austria   Brazil   Chile   Czech Republic   France   Greece
Guatemala   Hungary   Italy   Japan   Poland   Portugal   Singapore
South Korea   Switzerland   Thailand   Turkey   Ukraine   Vietnam

Published by Oxford University Press, Inc.
198 Madison Avenue, New York, New York 10016
http://www.oup.com

Oxford is a registered trademark of Oxford University Press

Library of Congress Cataloging-in-Publication Data

Goldschmidt, Walter Rochs, 1913-
  The bridge to humanity : how affect hunger trumps the selfish gene / Walter Goldschmidt.
    p. cm.
  Includes bibliographical references and index.
  ISBN 13: 978-0-19-517965-1 (alk. paper) – ISBN 13: 978-0-19-517966-8 (pbk. : alk. paper)
    ISBN 0-19-517965-X (alk. paper) – ISBN 0-19-517966-8 (pbk. : alk. paper)
    1. Evolutionary psychology. I. Title.

BF701.G58 2005
155.7–dc22   2004065464

Printing number: 9 8 7 6 5 4 3 2 1

Printed in the United States of America
on acid-free paper

For Natalie

Contents

Preface

This book shows how our hominid ancestors broke a fundamental law of evolution, namely, that every physical and behavioral trait of every living thing is ultimately motivated to maximize the survival advantage of its progeny, a rule that has come to be expressed in the phrase "the selfish gene." This transformation created a species capable of inducing individuals to behave in ways that run counter to this law; in fact, much human behavior lessens the chances of genetic success. This complex set of events, which gave impetus to a greater concern with sociality and made for the inevitable confrontation between self and other, makes a fascinating story, one that tackles one of the most important issues in the human sciences. The issue, that of "nature *versus* culture," here becomes "nature *and* culture"—leading to a debate with political as well as scientific implications. For you must understand that to know how we got here is also to know what we now are—which, in final analysis, is what we most want to know.

Affect hunger is the central character in the drama of this unique event. It is an inherent attribute in mammals, which must get affective response from their mothers in order to survive, an attribute that has long been known, although its full significance has not been recognized. How important it is in other mammals seems to vary, but it is quite important among primates and other social mammals, where its effects extend beyond close genetic kin. Affect hunger combined with the better-known traits of talking and making things to enable the world of culture to emerge, which is unique to our species.

Make no mistake; Homo sapiens is strictly one of a kind. We are an animal that is a product of the evolutionary process, and this unifies us with every other living creature. But the transformation I describe here led individuals to act in ways others want them to, and this enabled humans to have culture. This had the survival value of greater flexibility in behavior and gave us remarkable control over our own destiny. It did not extinguish the inherent animal urges, but it suppressed them or bent them to other purposes and redefined them as cultural rules. This flexibility led us to take over every terrestrial ecological niche useful to a large mammal without requiring further significant biological changes.

The story is not a simple one; affect hunger was combined with other inherent capacities to bring this revolutionary event about. It is complex, but neither mysterious nor difficult to understand. After an introductory chapter that sets the background, we examine our evolutionary heritage to discover the biological precursors we came with (chapters 2 and 3); then we will take a close look at the transition itself (chapters 4 and 5) and examine its outcome (chapters 6 and 7). Two concluding chapters explore broader implications.

An Appreciation of Evolution

I have never comprehended the difficulty people have understanding the theory of evolution. I find its story a far more compelling cosmology than any I have read in the vast mythic literature on the subject, and it is to me even more beautiful and soul-satisfying. Just the thought that we are one with all other beings now living in the world or that have ever lived over the billions of years since life emerged on the planet and that we share DNA and the whole machinery of inheritance with the mushroom and the butterfly, the elephant and the amoeba is to me a grand realization.

The details in this story offer parables about how we live and how we must live that are as intriguing as any to be found in sacred texts. Consider a few: Homo sapiens and *E. coli* show that even the greatest and very least of us are wholly dependent upon one another for our lives; giant whales swimming circles together like dancers to create an eddy that brings a concentration of krill so that each in turn can gulp a satisfying mouthful tell us that even the largest living mammals find gratification in cooperation; and, most of all, the fact that female mammals, whether the meekest mole or the fiercest queen of the jungle, along with our own mothers, have willingly—even eagerly—borne infants, who demand major sacrifices of them from conception until leaving home or lair (or even after), show how deeply nurturance is embedded in the mammalian lifestyle. These facts also remind us that evolution is not just "nature, red in tooth and claw," but that it also involves a large dose of mutuality.

Every cosmology must face the hardships and tragedies people must undergo and, most particularly, the inevitability of death. I find the efforts at denial of death less satisfactory than that which is inherent in the evolutionary process, which could not have taken place without the rhythms of birth and death. Change comes only as new generations acquire new traits that render the old obsolete. Had life emerged without this regeneration, there would only be strings of some kinds of unicellular forms that emerged from the primordial ooze and the planet would, at best, be covered with a blanket of the greens and grays of slime and mold. Understanding that others must have died for us to live and the inevitability that we must, in turn, die that others may live reinforces the sense of our continuity with eternity. Understandably, we shunt thoughts of death aside, but it is central to life and to evolution. This is part of another evolutionary truth: We must all eat to live, must take life to have life. In no other way could the earth support a continuing population—an integral and necessary part of the evolutionary process. So the very existence of our species has been made possible by the billions upon billions of beings who have died for us to get here, and we should remember this as we honor our own dead. It may not be as comforting as the imagination of an Edenic afterlife, but it honors our own existence.

Sometimes when I am relaxed and contemplating the wonderful road we took to get here, I conjure up an imaginative deity, an anthropomorphized—or, better, deified—evolutionary process. I call her Zoedora, giver of life, and think of her as a beautiful woman. I see her as a goddess who is responsible for most of the beauty and drama on this piece of cosmic dust; her knowledge, patience, and artistry transforming brute physical matter into the painterly landscapes all around us; her hands having framed the fearful symmetry of the tiger and created the grandeur of the elephant. She has taken energy from the sun to make birds that inscribe hundred-mile arcs in the sky and whales that swim from pole to pole. She can be profligate and a skinflint, wasting millions of sperm on each ejaculation but recycling everything. She started with nothing but raw materials and had to invent new kinds of matter to serve her creative aims. We think of gods as omnipotent and omniscient, but they must obey the laws of physics, making do with what they find here, constrained by what nature provides. Like the engineer, she had to cope with the pull of gravity and the force of winds; like the artist, she had to understand the refraction of light. I thought of us as her last great experiment. She was, however, a very human goddess. She had a feminine playfulness, as shown in the great collection of beetles she made and a kind of masculine hubris that led her to create the giant dinosaurs.

I was brought up short, however, when I realized I had given her the all-too-human quality of ambition—trying to create a creature that could evolve on its own. That was a teleological thought, and teleology is precisely what evolution is not. It was one of those dangers that lurk in metaphorical thought and led to a fallacy that was misleading. Adam Smith (an 18th-century philosopher whose *The Wealth of Nations* made him a founder of economics) had illustrated the mysteries of the marketplace as the outcome of myriad individual transactions by thousands upon thousands or persons engaging in exchange in the pursuit of profit and used the metaphor of the "unseen hand" as a way of accounting for it. Smith did not believe a hand was somewhere, nor would his readers, but it is a dangerous figure of speech for the evolutionary process, which so many want to attribute to a "grand design" shaped by some Unseen Hand. Evolution works like the marketplace works. It is the product of millions upon millions of generations of living beings, each reproducing itself and doing all it can to assure the survival of that progeny until they, in turn, can reproduce. No unseen hand causes evolution; there can be no Zoedora.

About This Book

This book is being written at the end of a long life devoted to anthropology, which has been a hobby almost as much as a career. It has taken me to study "stone age" tribes in northern California and the emergence of industrial agriculture further south in the same state. It has taken me to Africa, where I studied cultures in transition from cattle keeping to hoe-farming and saw the effects such disruption caused, as well as into the library stacks to find how such events related to the writing of others. All of my studies have been based on a perception of a triad of forces at work: *individuals* as independently self-motivated actors living in *societies* of many such individuals in mutual interdependence according to rules and customs that are their shared *culture*. My first theoretical work was *Man's Way* (1959), with its intentional double meaning, and my latest was *The Human Career* (1990), reiterating this pun; both anticipate in undeveloped form and marshal more evidence for what is more concisely presented here. I always ground theoretical discussion in the realities of social experience, and you will encounter Nomlaki, Hupa, and Tlingit activities to illustrate aspects of the story I develop here, along with the Sebei of Uganda and other East African people who underwent the trauma of technological changes that had occurred prior to colonialism, offering insight into the similar trauma that we nowadays suffer from technical changes. I like to exemplify every theoretical generalization with descriptions of actual events seen by me or reported by others. The breadth of knowledge covered in this volume has led me to call on data in areas where I have had no firsthand experience or long and intensive study; on these occasions, I have depended heavily on the expertise of others, citing their evidence and treading carefully.

Central to the whole is an understanding of affect hunger. I do not want to make it into a slogan, for slogans are the enemy of thought. It is not *the* key to understanding human society, but is the essential *missing* key. So it needs an exposition of its own, by which it can be strung on the chain of keys needed to open the doors to the scientific understanding of human behavior and the remarkable transition to humanity that, among other things, enables people like you and me to try to understand it. You will note that in the subtitle, I speak of it as "trumping" the selfish gene; the verb is carefully chosen, for it neither defeated it nor displaced it. While affect hunger has a kind of primacy in my view, it is not in control, but lives in tenuous relationship with the older sources of motivation.

Acknowledgments

A work of this scope coming at the end of a life owes so much to so many that it would not be possible or fair to try to name them. They extend from the family with which I spent my childhood to my professors at the Universities of Texas and California, whom I have recognized in earlier writings, to my present family and my late wife, Gale, who shared my research experience, to my colleagues and students at UCLA, and to those unseen and often unknown people whose writings have affected what I have said and thought, even when I disagree with them. Those who have given me help in the preparation of this manuscript are Mitch Allen, Geoffrey Clark, Sarah Hrdy, Michael Alan Park, Tom Weisner, and the faculty of the Center for Culture, Brain, and Development of the Foundation for Psychocultural Research at UCLA. I owe a special debt of gratitude to Jan Beatty of Oxford University Press for her conscientious editing and above all to Charles Merward, whose perceptive comments and discussions have had both tangible and subtle influences, and to his wife, Carlee Merward, who also helped in bringing this book into reality.

1

Nature *and* Nurture

Living things take form and engage in behavior that has been programmed in their genes and adapted, as a result of prior experience and ambient conditions, to the circumstances in which they find themselves. The basic lifestyle of each species is always inherited, but the degree and nature of this adaptability vary widely among living things, and this *variability is itself a genetic heritage.* Mammals appear to have more behavioral flexibility than other life-forms, and, among mammals, primates have the greatest plasticity; Homo sapiens is by far the most adaptable of all species. Adaptability is the hallmark of humanity, foreshadowed in our primate ancestry, as are so many of our special talents.

The Confrontation and Its Background

Just what in human behavior is set in our genetic heritage and what is responsive to accumulated experience is a major issue in understanding our species. The issue of nature versus nurture has divided scholars ever since science took over from theology the task of explaining what makes people behave as they do. Though it involves many disciplines, anthropology is this issue's natural habitat because it includes both orientations within its broadly defined borders. Though the dichotomy is as old as the discipline, it has become increasingly confrontational. Those whose specialized research leaves them unconcerned with general theory can

1

accept the formula that it is the nature of humans to have culture, but those of us who are involved with theory know that this begs the question. We will be looking at just what it means to say "it is in the nature of humans to have culture" in this book—that is, to explore the details of the interface between the two well-springs of human behavior.

It is of great importance to know what is set by our genes and what is amenable to social manipulation when formulating policy for such things as child care centers or retirement homes or when dealing with matters of education, criminal behavior, or substance abuse. When religions dominated our perceptions, their assumptions about human behavior shaped social policies, but as scientific studies began to invade the realm of human behavior in the 19th century, science inevitably invaded this territory, and biology-based assumptions were formulated in terms of "races," each treated as if it was a subspecies that had not evolved as far as ourselves. This ethnocentricity had great popular appeal—especially as Europeans had been colonizing, subordinating, and enslaving peoples in the newly "discovered" areas from which so many "people of color" came. Thus was born the myth of race, validated by anthropologists measuring physical features. Even those who saw humanity as one species explained differences in terms of an ethnocentric cultural evolution. Racial determinism dominated Western thought throughout the 19th century. Matters of "race" were front-and-center intellectual and public concerns when I was a student at the then racially segregated University of Texas, a state in which public policy was thoroughly racist. Even the anthropology department was divided, with one senior member a Southerner with racist assumptions and the other a French expat with egalitarian ones. We were taught the diverse efforts to classify the human races, all of which were based on visible physical features, but we also learned of the questionable evidence of black and "Caucasian" IQ differences. Even some of the more emancipated Texans still thought that "primitive languages" were unable to formulate abstract thought, which struck me as ludicrous, inasmuch as abstraction is essential to the formation of words.

The foundations of cultural theory were being laid down in the latter part of the 19th century by gentlemen scholars who explained the differences among people with a kind of teleological "progress"-oriented cultural evolution that tacitly assumed the superiority of European culture. The formulation of the modern concept of culture was made most explicit by Franz Boas, who came to the United States in 1884 with a German doctorate, a liberal secular Jewish background, and firsthand intimate experience among the Eskimo and Kwakiutl to join the faculty as professor of anthropology at Columbia University in the 1890s. From this base he launched and disseminated a school of thought that denied both racism and the ethnocentric cultural evolution of that time. His stance was that each people had a unique culture that was the product of its own unique history, which determined the thoughts and life patterns of its adherents. Early on, he attracted students, many of whom shared his German-American background and its personal experience with cultural diversity. With a strong belief in empirical data, he sent them into the field to make firsthand studies of native cultures and languages and then found posts for them in major universities across the country. Thus he established the dominance of the cultural paradigm in anthropology and cut into the racist assumptions found elsewhere in academia. His was more a philosophy than a theory, begging the fundamental question: Why the differences in culture?

The generation that came to maturity after World War I began to seek explanations that fell roughly into three categories: psychological, sociological, and ecological. The first was dominated by Freudian theory, then in its heyday, which provided the only comprehensive theory dealing with the factors affecting childhood behavioral development, a matter that could show how infants acquired the latent cultural traits from their parents to account for the continuity of culture. The second was influenced by French and German sociologists through the filter of British anthropologists and developed into what came to be called functionalism (later structuralism), which saw institutions as serving social needs. The third was more indigenously American, a neo-evolutionary thesis that saw cultures shaped by ecological adaptation rather than the teleological idea of progress. It does not take a genius to realize that these several schools of thought each have validity and were not really in conflict: The first attacked the matter of continuity, the second the problems culture had to solve, and the third how and why they differed. Nevertheless, they were highly confrontational, agreeing only in their rejection of biological explanations.

This gave an unreal *anti*-biological quality to anthropology. Meanwhile, the biological side in this division had largely abandoned the idea of race, though it lingered among scholars outside the field and lent a scientific aura in support of the continuing public prejudice.[1] Many physical anthropologists redefined themselves as biological anthropologists, moving from the physical to the behavioral aspects of humanity, getting their inspiration from the successive zoological schools of research on animal behavior—ethology, sociobiology, and evolutionary psychology. Ethology is the study of animal learning and behavior under natural conditions (in contrast to mazes) seeking to show the working of innate behavioral traits. Though an old field, it got its modern impetus from the work of Konrad Lorenz and Nikolaas Tinbergen shortly after World War II, who received the Nobel prize for their work. Anthropologists turned their attention to primates, largely pioneered by Sherbourn Washburn and given prominence by the dramatic studies on chimpanzees by Jane Goodall. Sociobiology was initiated by the entomologist E. O. Wilson, who did classic research on the social life of ants and set out to show the uniformities in animal social behavior, putting humans undifferentiated into the mix. Evolutionary psychology is the latest iteration of these efforts to see human behavior as biologically set by adaptation to the condition of our early hominid

---

1. The efforts have recently been summarized by Lee Baker in his review of books dealing with this problem (2004). The most prominent of these efforts to create a scientific racism was *The Bell Curve* (Herrnstein and Murray 1994). An effort to show that evolutionary psychology supported the theory of the inferiority of Africans was written by J. Philippe Rushton, a psychologist in Canada (1995). I received a complimentary copy, apparently courtesy of The Pioneer Fund, an organization that promotes "scientific racism," which sent out 30,000 summarizing pamphlets to anthropologists, psychologists, and sociologists, according to Baker.

existence. These movements did not reflect the earlier racist ideology, but they all made the assumption that genetic heritage was the only (or at least dominant) driving force in human behavior.

Anthropology has thus long embodied the duality that Snow identified in his famous "two cultures" essay (Snow 1959). It started as a combination of biology and humanitarian interests and became a social science by chance, as Alfred Kroeber pointed out long ago. At any rate, there really *are* two cultures in anthropology, one biological, the other humanitarian. The biological anthropologists are essentially hard science–oriented, mathematically literate, committed to research design and disposed to see the "hardware" as causative. They tend to feel more at home among biologists. Cultural anthropologists, standing somewhere between social science and the humanities, appreciate the force of ideas on human behavior and more often than not lack math skills but are at home with the ambiguities of human existence; they look for "understanding" rather than "causation." They are more congenial with humanists. In a later chapter I discuss the "engineer's logic" inherent in language as distinct from the "aesthetic sensibility" of other kinds of communication. The fact that these two cultures must live together, sharing budget, space, students, and curricular demands, makes departmental life difficult. Tensions are universal; newly created departments often try to avoid including both.

Public Interest in the Issue

The cultural perspective dominated anthropology for most of the 20th century in no small part because the racism that had suffused biological anthropology had become tainted by the growing awareness of the unspeakable Nazi excesses in its name. Cultural anthropology showed little awareness of the theoretical implications of the animal studies of Lorenz and Tinbergen, but when Wilson's *Sociobiology* (1975) came on the scene with extensive prepublication publicity, it created an uproar. His putting humans into the same mix with his ants and showing no awareness of culture was seen as a kind of neo-racism. (*Sociobiology* served as a bible for the neo-fascists in France for a while.) A few cultural anthropologists were drawn to sociobiology, but most were disturbed by its political implications. I was presiding over the meeting of the American Anthropological Association when a resolution was placed before it to "condemn the 'new synthesis' of sociobiology as an attempt to justify genetically the sexist, racist, and elitist status quo in human society" (American Anthropological Association 1976). Though I was not taken with Wilson's thesis, I fully agreed with Margaret Mead when she condemned the resolution as "nothing but book-burning" and was relieved when, after much parliamentary maneuvering, it was roundly defeated.

Mead was herself about to become the subject of a vicious attack. In 1983, five years after her death, Derek Freeman, a New Zealand cultural anthropologist who also had studied Samoan culture, denounced her cultural explanation of Samoan girls' sexuality (1983). Like Wilson, he got an unusual level of prepublication publicity, being featured on Phil Donahue's TV show, then perhaps the best nationwide book publicity available. Why all this attention to a questionable attack by a little-known anthropologist on the popularization of a dissertation by a 24-year-old woman discussing the sex lives of South Seas maidens written a half-century earlier? *Coming of Age in Samoa* (1961) was never part of the anthropological canon and was important only as a popularization of the culture-shapes-behavior thesis by the woman who had now become its poster child. The stir Freeman created had nothing to do with the quality of his scholarship, the cogency of his argument, or the salience of the subject matter; rather, it was an attack on cultural explanation. Anthropologists long ago wrote off Freeman's book, but the public press still cares. Freeman was immortalized before his death as the hero in a play produced in Wellington, New Zealand.

The most recent public attention to anthropology came as a result of an article in *The New Yorker* by Patrick Tierney (2000) that anticipated the thesis of his book, *Darkness in El Dorado* (2001). It deals with scholarly malfeasance among the Yanomamo, a people living in the Amazonian rain forest. Tierney was attacking the research program of James Neely, a geneticist, and Napoleon Chagnon, an anthropologist. It is Chagnon's work that is pertinent to our discussion. His *Yanomamö: The Fierce People* (1983) is a highly controversial and successful ethnography full of sex and violence. He says the Yanomamo are "fierce by nature." It has become a centerpiece for those involved with sociobiology, for it is the kind of flat generalization about human nature that they like, and his work is much cited by evolutionary psychologists. Chagnon, in an article in *Science* (1988), says that the fiercest men among the Yanomamo have more wives and more children than others and this proves that ferocity had "survival advantage" in the early stages of human evolution and that therefore aggression is just "human nature." Chagnon's work has been attacked on all levels: methodology, validity of the data, and the reality of the correlations. But these matters are essentially irrelevant, for the argument itself is spurious. No single society can represent the original human society, as we shall see later, most particularly not the Yanomamo, who are *horticulturalists,* not the foragers who are usually considered the ur-condition of humanity. There were no letters of objection published in response to his article. Of course, I don't know how many were submitted, but my own letter to *Science* was rejected solely on the basis of Chagnon's totally inadequate refutation—an unprofessional, strange, and arrogant procedure. One might argue that the elite, however they get there, will always have the most progeny, but even this is not true. Consider the Hupa and Yurok *foraging* societies that we will meet later and who (like ourselves) give up having many children in the pursuit of other values. Being foragers, would they not be a better model for the human ur-condition?

These controversies display the strange public involvement with anthropology. Freeman has been canonized; the editor of *Science* (whose credentials were not likely to have been in the behavioral sciences) places his judgment of Chagnon's thesis above that of an established anthropologist; journalists take delight in twitting anthropologists for their disputes, reducing them to foibles and thus trivializing the issues that evoke these controversies. Their reactions to Tierney were not deterred by ignorance. The editorial sections of both the *New York Times* and the *Los Angeles Times* of October 8, 2000, each had a column using the Yanamamo issue to attack anthropology as a discipline (though, ironically, they adhered to opposite sides). Daniel Zalewski's

"Anthropology Enters the Age of Cannibalism" in the *New York Times* (2000) focused, as the title implies, on anthropological infighting; it was a virulent, uninformed support of biological determinism. Alexander Cockburn's (2000) "What Happens When Genocide Poses as Science" pays no attention to the issues raised by Tierney or Chagnon but attacks anthropology for its alleged indifference to the conditions of the Native Americans by citing out-of-context references to things Alfred Kroeber had said nearly a century earlier. Judith Shulevitz (2001) in the *New York Times Book Review* is bemused at the infighting in a field that "has no reason to exist" because it is "an enterprise that began as a Victorian gentlemen's hobby"—oblivious to anthropology's deep roots in 19th-century German science, French philosophy, and the American frontier. As Alexander Pope said, "a little learning is a dangerous thing."

Such public involvement with anthropology is not new. The finds of hominids made in the 19th and early 20th centuries were often hotly disputed in the public press and even among scholars, based on religious belief, nationality, or regional loyalties. The infamous "Piltdown hoax," in which an ape jaw together with an old-looking human cranium was placed in an old streambed in England, was motivated by the desire to have the island included in the early history of humanity. (I was never taken in by this because my Francophonic anthropology professor was, not without some ethnic loyalty of his own, dubious of the find, an attitude that ultimately proved correct.) This is only the most dramatic manifestation of the public involvement in such matters. They show how important it is to get it right.

Reading the adversaries in the conflict between the biologically oriented and culturally oriented scholars, one cannot escape feeling that they each have such a strong vested interest in their position that any compromise is seen as heresy—not unlike religious fundamentalists' attitude toward ecumenicalism. This is not fortuitous for, as with religion, each sees his view as being the truth that will guide him to heaven or, at least, to the right social policies. My own interest in finding the middle ground is not innocent of the latter purpose.

Toward a Resolution of the Conflict

Manifestly, this is not an either/or issue, but a matter of interrelationship. Data are at hand to show how the biological and the cultural interact, and I shall here outline the evolutionary process that brought this about. The old clichés and sound-bite ideas such as "social instinct" or "determinant genetically inherited traits" are not sufficient to account for the absolutely unique product of the evolutionary process that is Homo sapiens and the wide diversity in its behavior over space and time. Rather, we must formulate an orderly picture built on the research findings drawn from all of anthropology's subfields and beyond to include child development studies, brain research, and psychology, among others. This means that we must look more deeply at the actualities of our biological background, at the true dynamics of the evolutionary process, and most particularly at what goes on in the brain and the body chemistry that leads to our unique end product, a being that challenges the priority of the imperatives of species survival.

2

Heritage from the Distant Past

All living things are part of a continuous efflorescence of life-forms through the flow of genes, a continuum from the very beginning of life on this planet with successive mutations that made change possible. Favorable mutations improve the chance for survival in an ever-changing environmental context for generation after generation of progeny—an eternal reiterative sequence of ecological adaptations. The constant iteration over a billion or so years has made for the great diversity of life-forms and their spread over the face of the earth. In the course of this history, several of these forms have become increasingly complex, and this has led to the popular perception of evolution as being progressive. This complexity is an epiphenomenon—the secondary consequence of the evolutionary process. It comes about because each change adds to the total possibilities available to later generations, not because they replace the simpler ones, though they may also do that. We humans are the culmination of one particular line of development—primates most dependent upon the use of their brain—that is just one of the many sequences to be found in evolutionary efflorescence. For all this continuity, it is still the case that our species is seen as unusually unique, taxonomically, in that it has been placed as the only living species in the genus but also in the family in the classic *Walker's Mammals of the World* (Nowak and Paradiso

1983).[1] This, as we shall see, is a by-product of the adaptability of our ancestry as it invaded and controlled all the available ecological niches useful to large terrestrial mammals. For all the talk about there being only a 2 percent difference between humans and chimpanzees, we are far apart in our physical attributes as well as our behavioral potentials, and this is what is reflected in classic taxonomy.

Darwin did not invent the idea of evolution; indeed, that can better be attributed to his grandfather, Erasmus Darwin. What Charles Darwin did was to show, by careful, controlled, and repeated experimentation, that one species could morph into another when certain environmental differentials gave some an advantage by dint of some altered ability or physical feature. These differentials could be spatial, as was the situation on the Galapagos Islands where the fauna so intrigued him, as well as temporal. It was the inheritance of such adaptive improvements for survival in the competition for getting sustenance and mates that is the prime mover in the process; the general assumption is that the acquisition of the more adaptive traits are chance occurrences through "genetic mutation," which are then selected for. Popular writings sometimes recast the process dramatically as "survival of the fittest," which emphasizes the competitive aspect or sees it as a teleological development toward some predetermined end, such as ourselves. I see the manifest evidence of the increased complexity of life as a secondary consequence of the simple fact that the more complexity that exists at any one time, the greater the complexity possible.

We must take note of one other aspect of the evolutionary process, namely, that the adaptations that take place are always

---

1. Modern specialists in human evolution have rejected this classification based upon gene similarities, but, especially in light of the uncertainties in the interpretation of such data, it does not seem appropriate to base classification of hominids on separate criteria. In final analysis, taxonomies rest on judgment, and I find this revisionism an effort to minimize human uniqueness. I return to this issue later.

built on what is already there. The obvious analogy is to remodeling a house. What one can do is always affected by what is already there, and while the end result may be a great improvement, it might have been better if it had not been necessary to accommodate preexisting conditions. When remodeling a house, one can destroy some of the existing structure, but the evolutionary process does not have this option. To be sure, features of a species can be eliminated and often have been, but the basic plan can only change by the same incremental process that applies to evolution as a whole, each increment building on what had gone before. For this reason, the end product is not always the best that can be imagined, but only the best remodeling that could be achieved. These strictures also apply to the cultural evolution we examine in chapter 7.

The Issue of the "Selfish Gene"

The prime mover of this evolutionary process can be seen as a "motive"[2] that is built into all living creatures, the motive to do the things that will increase the probability of passing genes to the next generation—that is, to do what enhances selectability (Dawkins 1989). The inherent press for continuity must have been the first hereditary trait established in living things, for without this urge, evolution could not take place. It is a logical necessity without any empirical evidence other than the possibility to note that all—or practically all—physical and behavioral features of plants and animals can be shown to contribute to such an end. In this sense, the evolutionary process resides in the individual and each individual is in competition with all others to further its heritage as against those of its rivals, though it often does so by collaboration with others in herds, schools, swarms, and the like, or with other species in symbiosis.

The emergence of an animal that will take actions that do not fit this formula is therefore a special problem in evolutionary theory.

---

2. Of course this is not a motive in the sense of intent on the part of the individual being.

How did nature manage to select for an animal that will sacrifice its life for others? Of course, if those others share all or a large fraction of its genes, as when protecting its own offspring or pregnant mate, there is no problem. But humans regularly sacrifice themselves for others, even for abstract principles. It is this bridge our ancestry crossed; it is this transition that is central to this work.

As my title indicates, I see affect hunger as an essential key to this transformation. It is not the only one, but it is a crucial and neglected element in a long and complicated process. Affect needs were identified by Abraham Maslow (1968:381) as "love and affection and belongingness needs" that come into play after the needs for safety and physiological functions have been met. Mark Solms and Edward Nersessian (1999) point out that Freud's treatment of affect is embedded in his perception of the whole mental apparatus in its service to the imperative internal needs of the individual. These needs, Freud tells us, are met through drives that do the work of responding to them, a process regulated by the "pleasure principle." The successful meeting of the inner needs— a quantitative reduction in the drive pressure—is felt qualitatively as pleasure. As we shall see, these concepts are beginning to get a physical reality in the form of specific chemical or electrical activity in the brain.

Fundamental Elements for Humanity

Our species inherited three major characteristics from its mammalian ancestry that deserve our special attention.

1. *Control of body temperature.* One of these is the ability to control our internal body temperature. This reduced dependency on external sources of energy and enabled mammals (and birds, who share this trait) to live, with appropriate mutations, in almost every earthly environment. As the fundamental advantage in having culture lies in adaptability, this gave our species the flexibility to adjust to extremely hot and extremely cold climates by making behavioral adaptations and not requiring significant genetic mutations.

2. *Live birth.* The second major behavioral characteristic is that complex of features that made viviparous birth possible. These

include the uterine feeding of the embryo through the mother's blood, the eponymous mammary glands by which to nurture the newborn, and the extended infantile dependency that this requires. Unlike most vertebrates that are born as fully formed miniature versions of adults, mammals are born as immature beings, dependent upon their parents to bring them up to speed until they can fend for themselves. This unusual pattern of dependence involves all mammals in some degree of social life, with an inborn capacity for mutual support, enabling—actually requiring—bonds to be forged between parent and offspring and among siblings.

3. *Sociality.* Consistent mutual interaction among conspecifics—social life—runs throughout the animal world. Students of evolution like to emphasize the competitive aspect of animal behavior—the survival of the fittest—and play down the role of affinity in the daily lives of living things. Competition is important but mutuality is equally so. Mushrooms are formed by millions of separate individually viable spores, single-cell bits of life, each of which is capable of reproduction but all "collaborating" to form towers that give a greater chance for the reproductive success of their common genome. Mutuality is shown in schools of fish, flocks of birds, and swarms of insects, suggesting that mutuality has survival value, even though the nature of this mutuality is not always clear nor its function necessarily always the same. The most elaborate forms of social life in the animal kingdom are those of the social insects. They evolved three separate times—ants, termites, and bees. Each used the same trick to solve the evolutionary problem of subordinating individual selectivity to group survival—namely, making the hive or colony the unit of natural selection. This was achieved by having each hive consist of individuals with much the same genetic makeup and by allocating the business of reproduction to small selected sectors of the community. Disengaged from reproduction, each rank-and-file ant, termite, or bee has no competitive urge vis-à-vis one another—only against rival hives. Mammalian sociality is built on parenting. Central to this parenting are the affective ties between the parents and their offspring.

We are only beginning to learn of the physiology involved in this parenting, but we do know there are mechanisms that program both parental and neonate behavior and that provide the physiological underpinnings of this essential mammalian behavior. They offer clues to the biological reality of affect hunger. The fact that tactile stimuli (licking, grooming, and caressing) are necessary for the proper growth of the neurons was the first clear evidence of a physiological role in what appears merely to be social behavior. We now know that peptides program diverse parenting behavior in different mammals. We return to this matter later.

Human parenting did not eliminate the individual sexuality with its inherent competitiveness. Mammalian reproduction requires at least intermittent social interaction between males and females and extended interaction between mothers and offspring. This is the extent of the social life for some species, but these ties of affinity and consanguinity are often built upon to create larger units of collaboration. Adult males may be involved and sibling bonds may be formed, continuing to play a role in adult animal behavior. Elephant society, for instance is built around mother–daughter and sister–sister bonds. The all-important parental relationship, together with the mating bond, where it exists, forms the basis on which many mammalian social systems are built. Parental care began with some dinosaurs (for which there is some paleontological evidence), and birds engage in it, though they perform it differently. Collaboration may be no more than the passive safety in numbers of ungulate herds, but it can also form the basis of active mutual protection, group feeding, and even food sharing. Strong social ties are usual among primates and are often important among the canines, elephants, the lions among cats, and at least some cetaceans and rodents. The actual social organization varies from species to species depending on its inherent lifestyle and situational ecology.

Nonhuman primate social organization varies widely. The mating bond and parent–offspring ties can be built to form large communities of mutual support or can remain as separately operating family groups; sometimes mating involves bonding, but sexual promiscuity also occurs. Some monkeys push males out of local bands to avoid inbreeding; others push the females out; still others manage not to push either out. This variation in social relationships among our nearest kin make it impossible to find the model out of which human social organization might have emerged—a search that largely inspired primate studies by anthropologists. Ecological conditions apparently account for the size and nature of primate social groups. Under appropriate conditions localized bands include individuals that have no recognizable genetic ties, showing that primate predilection for social behavior can support at least minimally adequate harmony and mutual protection against the threat of reproductive rivalry. No nonhuman animals are known to have social groups that extend beyond the locality; indeed, it is hard to see how they could be formed in the absence of a symbolic world, and this requires language. I have illustrated this diversity by listing the behavioral differences between chimpanzees and bonobos, two closely related species of the genus most closely related to us (see Sidebar 1). These differences are so much involved with basic outlook that we might say that they differ in ethos. One is tempted to engage in an experiment, like one that Hans Kummer (1971) did on baboons to see if the differences were a learned practice or a genetic difference.[3] It is interesting to compare these differences in the Pan genus with variation among foragers shown in Sidebar 13.

Learning

These behavioral attributes required a quantum leap in the development of learning. Learning is not limited to mammals but it has taken on much greater saliency among them, enabling experience to be transmitted from one living being to another. Such transmission may merely be incidental but it also may be consciously initiated (that is, taught) among the more social mammals. Culture

---

3. Kummer was studying two closely related baboon species, one in which males closely herded the females and the other in which they did not and transferred some females from one to the other. He found that they adapted with difficulty, but could change their behavior in accordance with their new social context.

BEHAVIORAL VARIATION WITHIN THE GENUS *PAN*

Item	Chimpanzee	Bonobo
Bands	Mostly all-male groups	Few all-male groups
	Border control by fighting	No border fighting
Male–female relationships	Female alliances based on kin	Female alliances attack males
	Males and females often separate	Sexes remain together more
	Males control desirable food and females beg from males	Females control desirable food and do not beg
	Weaker ties to mother	Stronger ties to mother
Sexual behavior	Copulation shorter, less often, and more discreet	Copulation longer, more often, and more open
	Sex by mounting and dorsal entry	Sex face to face with eye contact
	Same-sex sexual contact not observed	Both males and females make same-sex genital contact
Tools and food	Much tool-using activity	Little tool-use observed
	More game hunting	Little game hunting
General observations	Appears to be more in-ternalized self-control and more hostility and social conflict	Appears to be more re-laxed social interaction and less social control

Falk 2000, Chapter 13.

is, by definition, learned behavior, rendering learning crucial to the evolution of the human condition.

Academics, who owe their tenure to the evidence that they excel in learning, if not in teaching, tend to think that learning is an unalloyed virtue. Most living things, however, have little use for learning. Learning stands in contrast to hard-wired genetic determinism; it fine-tunes behavior to situational demands. For all of its ultimate value to humanity, learning can be seen to be a mixed blessing. It offers the advantage of adaptability at the cost of certainty and speed of response. Which need is the greater varies with what the animal is engaged in and so plays a greater role among some animals than others. For instance, it is more important for predators to learn tricks of the chase than for their prey, who rely on instant response. (The musings of Hamlet are not conducive to a quick getaway, while forethought may help in choosing the strategy for an aggressive act.) Learning is more important to social mammals than solitary ones, for they must learn to take cues from one another.

Learning is made possible by an often unattended aspect of the genetics of behavior, namely, that there is a gap between the encoded genetic instruction and behavioral performance. Those who deal with the development of the brain, where it is particularly important, call this "neuroplasticity," but, as it has more general implications, I like to call it "genetic indeterminacy." The need for licking or grooming to make the dendrites and neurons grow to their full potential is an example of such genetic indeterminacy. Geneticists are fully aware of this phenomenon, but those who popularize genetics do not give indeterminacy adequate attention even though it is implicit in the very fact that most genes that are said to *cause* a disease actually just increase the *probability* of its occurrence; that is, genetic inheritance is not causative but a contributing factor. Genetic indeterminacy is open-ended and not to be confused with delayed manifestation of traits, such as those that cut in at sexual maturation. As we begin to learn about the mechanisms involved in the transmission of culture and the role of affect hunger, we find this adaptive gap in the transmission of behavior to be of vital importance. We will come back to this phenomenon, for it is crucial to understanding the transition from biological determination to the behavioral adaptability of humans.

Learning comes in different forms. Imprinting, with set responses to set cues, is learning at its cheapest and may not even be seen as learning. Some human learning comes so readily as to seem like imprinting; we learn to fear snakes more readily than more modern dangers, presumably an atavistic trait from the past.

This example shows that the very idea of tabula rasa—the idea that our brains are like unexposed film capable of any action—is ridiculous. This pre-adaptation to learning certain kinds of things applies to most of what gives humanity its special character, for it is of dramatic importance to learning language, as we shall see.

The viviparous birth of incompletely formed mammalian infants condemns them to a period of dependency in which they not only gain in strength and ability but also learn much of what they are to do as adults. Humans have the longest period of such dependency; this enables them to undergo the very long period of instruction that is necessary for transmitting culture. It is reasonable to assume that affect hunger came into being as a reward system to ensure the attention of infants and children to the demands of their caretakers as they were being taught to behave in ways their community wanted them to. Affect needs appear among social animals other than primates and so must be an old mammalian trait.

Our Ancient Heritage

The path that led to the formation of a primate dominated by culture began long before there were any primates; it involved the urge for community inherent in mammalian procreation, the dependency that enabled adults to transmit knowledge, and the ability of the neonate to absorb it, enabling us to live in communities.

The following syllogism gives a kind of summation of the lesson this chapter has provided, and we will apply it to the evidence of how our hominid ancestry built upon this to create the tools that were essential to the formation of beings that would live in so large a measure by their own wits.

- Many genetic instructions that make us human are indeterminate, requiring fine adjustments.
- These adjustments are responses to situational conditions.
- The actions of other humans create some situational conditions.
- Therefore, social and biological cannot be separate realms.

3

Tools for the Transition

Einstein said he did not believe that God played dice—but in fact the evolutionary process does gamble. Evolution laid its chips on intelligence against brute strength when, ten or so million years ago, primates began down the path that ultimately led to us.

The Evolutionary Gamble

Consider what was laid on the line. The tried-and-true quadrupedal stance was sacrificed for a tenuous bipedalism that involved making a not very satisfactory S-shaped spine on which a large, hard head was balanced. This not only required elaborate reorganization of the feet but also disrupted the internal organs by hanging them from a pole rather than a rod, so to speak. The other major structural change was to increase the size of the cranium relative to the body to make room for an expanding brain that needed more space for smarts than muscles. This was a costly investment, not only because the brain is expensive tissue to maintain and operate, but also because it involved giving up much fighting effectiveness (strong, prognathous jaw; sharp, projecting canines; and acuity in the sense of smell) to make room for it. Even worse, the large cranium made it hard and dangerous for mothers to give birth. Upright posture did little or nothing to enhance brute effectiveness; on the contrary, it increased vulnerability and made no effort to compensate for the losses by arming the forelimbs for combat. What came in return are a greater computing capacity, a flexible forelimb good for throwing, and a remarkable, delicately muscled hand capable for manipulating and grasping.

Put this way, it seems obvious that all these changes were selected to progressively enhance the ability of humans to outsmart their potential prey or predators and ultimately led them not only to use tools and weapons found in nature but also to make them, culminating in the intelligence that gave them an advantage over physical forms of aggression and defense. This trade-off seems inadequately appreciated in the discourse on our evolutionary development. The essential product of these physical alterations was the creation of a mind and body capable of doing the two things that distinguish Homo sapiens from all other forms of life: talking and making things. These, together with the forelimbs and skull that made them possible, are the two things that, more than anything, differentiate the humans species from all other forms of life, both physically and behaviorally. It is reasonable to think that these two talents came as a package and evolved together, each an essential player in this co-evolution. In fact, the mental processes involved in speaking and in making things are essentially alike.

I am convinced that this evolution took place before our species came into being and am impressed with the argument that renowned South African paleoanthropologist Philip Tobias has made that language appeared with the emergence of the genus *Homo*. Tobias has argued since 1980 that our first ancestor to use language was *Homo habilis* and ties this directly to the tool-making of this early member of our genus. He recently (2003) summarized his reasoning by noting the

> remarkable approximate contemporaneity between (1) the first known appearance of the modern human cerebral sulcal pattern [in the brain], (2) the first known emergence of the parts of the brain that govern spoken language, (3) the first appreciable enlargement of the hominid brain, (4) the first appearance in the archaeological record of deliberately fashioned stone tools and (5) signs of cooling, drying and elevation, i.e., overall deterioration of Africa's environment [as a pressure for adaptive change].

He goes on to suggest that there was a positive feedback between the increased complexity of the material culture and the enlargement and reorganization of the brain. An examination of the mental processes involved in making things and in talking displays a correspondence in the gross mental activity involved; that is, a case of identical form; of being isorphormic. Before we can examine this, we must consider the mental tricks that enter into human speech.

The Relevance of Human Speech to Tool-Making

The three major behavioral elements involved in human speech are (1) the articulation of delicately nuanced sounds, (2) the formulation of conceptual categories, and (3) structuring the relation among the elements brought together in utterances. (Sounds, words, and grammar, respectively, in popular parlance.)[1]

The delicate, precise, and rapid muscular control of the vocal cords, lips, mouth, and breath involved in making the rapid succession of sounds that go into the everyday use of speech is an unusual (perhaps unique) physical/mental capability. These articulated sounds are very different from anything made by other primates in their extensive "vocabularies," or by other mammals. The vocalizations of birds are perhaps the most demanding alternative; birds' ability to imitate us suggests that they have the capability, if not the dexterity or the mental capacity, for using vocal speech. (My use of this word "dexterity," with its etymological basis in the manipulation of the fingers, itself evokes the similarity between talking and manipulating.) It is not irrelevant that the efforts to teach the apes to speak had to give up the use of sound as the medium for their communication, though I agree with researchers on ape "speech" that the sound system is not crucial to mental capacity for human speech. The pattern of delicate and precise use of the muscles and their transformation from conscious effort to a kind of kinesthetic automation are characteristic of both talking and fabrication.

The second general feature of human language is the formulation of "morphemes," the linguists' term for what we think of as

---

1. I am avoiding the terminology of the linguists who are concerned with more nuanced problems; here I want to focus on the basic gross character of the speech phenomenon.

words. Most of any vocabulary consists in terms for things, actions, or attributes that are available to sensory perception—or are seen to be. (The rest do the work of grammar, discussed next.) These morphemes are not merely labels of things, they are labels of *categories* of things, actions, or attributes. The trick was to transform the confusion of sensory perceptions of the universe and its workings into classes of objects, actions, or attributes that are each bounded and distinct from all others. This mental act requires that the relevant entity not only be separated from background or context to become a thing in itself but also be recognized as the member of a class based on some latent taxonomic principle. Thus, the specifics of the stick in the hand (or the color of it or the throwing of it) are examples of a universe of sticks (or attributes or actions). Whether it is an explicit thing, like our stick, or imaginary (as a ghost), an idea (causation, for instance) or an undifferentiated mass (sand or water), the language must treat it as an example of a categorical entity. This transforms the four-dimensional universe that is a continuous and unbroken whole into finite bits and pieces—like a giant pot shattered into millions of shards. Each language has broken the pot in its own way, so that the pieces from one do not always match those of another, as every translator knows. All human languages do this, for it is an essential part of the genius of speech, but, significantly, they do not all formulate the same entities. Whether this ability is unique to humans is not known, but some animals apparently learn to recognize categories of things in nature, as, for instance, the dog seeking a grass that will serve as an emetic or the chimpanzee finding a twig for fishing termites.

These examples suggest a fundamental similarity between speech and making things, namely, that a person has a font of words to choose from when he wants to formulate a sentence just as someone making something has a font of raw materials out of which to make it, a classification that separates the appropriate available material from the inappropriate for the project at hand. However much the actions may differ, the mental processes involved in having and being able to use an inventory of things or a lexicon of words available are, it seems to me, quite isomorphic.

The third mental process in human speech is grammar, that is, the rules by which these separate entities are put together to make a meaningful utterance. This is the element that is truly unique to human communication. In human speech, the speaker must select items from the universe of known units in the local lexicon and string them together according to local rules in a way that shows how each relates to the others in an utterance. The local rules involve those other morphemes mentioned earlier and the sequencing of the chosen elements that form what we call grammar and syntax. Just as the labels vary from one language to another, so do the rules for defining their relationship in a sentence. Every competent speaker must learn the words that are labels and must also learn the rules for their meaningful articulation. There is every reason to believe, as Noam Chomsky (whose seminal contribution we discuss later) pointed out many years ago, that humans are endowed with some special mental capacity for learning these rules through experiencing their use by those around them. This capacity to learn grammar without conscious effort is limited to a brief window of opportunity as the child grows so that one who never hears human speech before puberty is forever incapable of learning grammar; yet those who have learned one system can learn other languages, but, as most of us know, this requires diligence and work. This universal procedure establishes the *universality* of the talent while enabling the *diversity* of actual performance, making language *adaptable*. The animal precedent for this is the widely, if not universally, found ability of newborn mammals to learn the smell, sound, or sight of its own mother—an inherent general ability used with experiential particulars.

The capacity for using grammar and syntax is unique to humans and differentiates our speech from all other known forms of animal communication. The valiant efforts to teach apes to speak have shown their great ability to learn, to handle symbolization (or at least representation), and their capacity to communicate, but none of them has learned even the rudiments of grammar. They have occasionally strung together enough of the "lexical" units in ways that can be interpreted as syntax but none has ever communicated information about events outside the immediate time and place where the event occurred. No ape can formulate a communication in such a way as to separate itself from the subject matter of the discourse. All animal communication is essentially egocentric, even where it has a social purpose, as with warning calls. Grammar frees communication from ties to the immediate time and place; neither person, object, nor the action in the utterance need to be present when it is made. This disengagement lets speech create the narratives that can be detached from the persons communicating. This capability is essential to the creation of culture, as we see in a later chapter.

Meanwhile, I point out again, putting a sentence together is not unlike making things, for it involves drawing items from an inventory of known raw materials in the environment, while putting them together in an orderly fashion is like the syntax of a sentence. And, to carry the homology further, the mastic and cord to bind parts together is like the phonemes and declensions that are used to bind the parts of a sentence into a whole.

The reasoning underlying making things that is also implicit in syntax was acquired some time between the hominids' occupation of Olduvai about 1.3 million years ago and the existence of those who scattered the artifacts that littered the ground in Isimila some million years later, according to the analysis by Thomas Wynn (1979). (Olduvai is the gorge in Tanzania where Louis and Mary Leakey found so many of the remains of our early ancestors and their crude artifacts; Isimila is on the plains not far away that were scattered with hundreds of Lower Paleolithic stone tools when I was there in 1961.) By examining carefully the flaking on the artifacts, Wynn figured that the Olduvai tools could have been made by hit or miss but that the Isimila ones could only have been made by an orderly sequence of blows to achieve their preconceived form. This implies a whole new level of intellectual ability.

These Lower Paleolithic hominids not only shaped stones to a plan, but also had, as we might expect, a wood-working industry as well. Two well-made javelins and some other wooden artifacts of uncertain use found in a coal mine at Schröningen, Germany (Thieme 1997), demonstrated the existence of sophisticated craftsmen. Each spear "is made from the trunk of a 30-year-old spruce tree; in each, the end with the tip comes from the base of the trunk, and each has the same proportions with the centre of gravity a third way from the sharp end, as in a modern javelin" (Dennell 1997). Their detailed likeness shows that the artisan had a taxonomy of trees in mind, and I suspect he was capable of articulating it.

On the Origin of Language

The hoary topic of language origins needs renovation. Received wisdom nowadays seems to favor the idea that it evolved out of animal vocalizations and gestures. My belief is that its origin required a special growth of the brain, as Tobias thought when he examined *Homo habilis,* and thus emerged in conjunction with the making of artifacts.

Communication between separate living entities is so widespread that one might believe it to be a universal attribute of animal life. Communication takes many forms: auditory, tactile, olfactory, visual, and possibly others for which our species has no organs for sensory reception. Communication takes place not only between members of the same species but also between those of different species and even between plants and animals—and, for that matter, even between the organs of the body. Some of the modes of communication between animals may be learned, as perhaps are the vervet calls and birdsongs. Vervet calls are intriguing because they offer a kind of taxonomy of vervet sources of danger, just as bee-dancing is special because it refers to something that is out of sight. Yet even these communications make reference only to immediate, existing conditions, and almost all of them signal the state of mind (more accurately, and not insignificantly, mood) of the sender: lust, threat, fear. None of them is capable of placing utterances in time or space or offering conditions or contingencies; all deal only with the here and now.

The partial success of a number of researchers to get apes to use signs and computer icons to express themselves have shown that these primates can attach meanings to a variety of symbols and use them in meaningful ways to transmit a message. This has given a lot of publicity and some credence to the theory that human language is directly descended from the mental capabilities of the ancient animal calls and gestures. There are many difficulties with this thesis, however, the greatest of which has already been noted—namely, the failure to teach apes even the fundamentals of grammar; that is, apes cannot disengage the message from the messenger. Apes cannot express thoughts that live independently from those in direct communication.

There are other objections. I noted at the outset that giving primacy to the mind over physical prowess was a costly choice. My thesis sees language as almost a secondary result, a handmaiden, if you will, to the growth of the ability to make tools and weapons, which offers an obvious survival advantage, an advantage that can grow with each incremental advance in technology. The importance of speaking over passive learning by imitation becomes particularly clear when applied to making things wherever collaboration between individuals is involved. It is also the case that gestures and calls in other animals deal with emotional states, as noted earlier, while speech primarily deals with matters of cognition. The suggestion has been made that verbal language has an advantage over gestures and calls in preserving and restoring social harmony and so got its survival value in promoting the social order. I have seen no evidence for this; my experience is that personal conflict always involves the emotions that are notably difficult to convey with speech and that, more often than not, talking exacerbates conflicts while gestures and even meaningless cooing sounds often placate them.

Upright posture, though not directly related to the origin of speech, was necessary for altering the forelimbs to create the hands with which people make things. It has been argued that added height, offering a larger visual field, gave survival value, but this hardly seems an adequate payoff for the costs involved, having been achieved by bears and prairie dogs more simply.

An article in *Science* recently addressed the origin of language. It set forth a thesis that human speech is a subset of a more generalized "language faculty" (Hauser et al. 2002). The authors do not tell us what is to go into this broader category, for they don't examine the full range of communication found in nature. If we put the dancing of bees and the singing of birds together with ape calls and gestures into a construct that includes human speech, then why not also the pheromones of the ants or the means of communication (whatever it may be) that enables fish to join schools or birds to fly in formation? We can go on to include the clear messages between organs of the body that appear as pangs of hunger or sexual arousal and, speaking of sex, the smells and colors used by flowers to entice the bees to pollinate. If, on the other hand, the authors mean only to deal with primate communication, then they still must face another problem. For humans have two forms of communication, not counting the "body language," facial expressions, and olfactory signals we regularly send, without even intending to. Later I set forth the case for our forebears having harnessed the gestures and cries of our primate ancestors to make music and dance into a second "language" that we call ritual. This is better suited to the communication of affect than knowledge, for language deals better with factual matters than with sentiment.

To be sure, languages do co-opt the sounds and gestures of our primate ancestry. We regularly embellish our talk with intonation, gesture, and exclamation; we fancy it up with poetry, song, and figures of speech that help to communicate feelings. We also draw on the scoldings and cursings reminiscent of animal discourse. It amuses me that monkeys use copulatory "presenting" and "mounting" positions as a way to show submission and dominance, just as we do metaphorically with certain vulgar words and phrases, as well as less explicit gestures, giving these primate gestures the equivalence of figures of speech. These examples show that there is a continuity in the use of gestures between apes and humans, but they are embellishments to grammatical speech and not the essence of it.

Language and the Brain

The *Science* article referred to in the last section offers the theory that there is a "language faculty" in the human brain. This notion of a language organ is out of keeping with modern neurology. The old belief that each person's brain was set out early in ontological development and was thereafter immutable has slowly given way to the realization that the brain is subject to changes in shape and internal organization in response to environmental conditions. Elizabeth Bates and F. Dick (2002) say that "the neural mechanisms that participate in language still do other kinds of work, but they have grown to meet the language task." They go on to say that "there may be something special about the human brain that makes language possible, but that 'something' may involve highly distributed mechanisms that serve many other functions." This is the recognition that the brain is a volatile and adaptive organ, not the housing for separate functional organs, as is the case with the many functions involved in the processing of food in the intestinal tract.

We have been given some insight into the workings of the brain by the discovery of "mirror neurons." Animal calls are thought to be processed in the limbic system, that ancient part of the brain that deals with emotions such as fear, lust, and anger, but human speech is processed in two areas of the cerebrum, that part of the brain that demanded the enlarged skulls of humanity. This perception is supported by a recent discovery of a new set of neurons. A group of scientists in Italy discovered a brain activity they called mirror neurons, which offers scientific support for my theory that language emerged in conjunction with the making of artifacts. The team had been studying motor neurons in the F5 area in the macaque brain. These motor neurons encode movement in quite abstract terms, especially regarding the relation between the animal and the object of its action. Motor neurons become active only if an action, such as grasping or holding, is executed to achieve a particular goal, such as picking up or throwing away something like a piece of food. The metaphor of a "motor vocabulary" has been used to conceptualize these functions, for they offer a kind of "vocabulary" of motor acts, making it simpler to select and perform a particular action. With a motor "vocabulary," motor action can be conceived as an assembly of words, as being a more economical control of individual movements. Such an experiment was in progress when the mirror neurons were discovered (see Sidebar 2).[2] As of this writing, more than 30 articles have been published on mirror neuron research.

The F5 area of the macaque brain, in which mirror neurons appear, evolved into Broca's area in humans, the language area that controls lip and tongue movement. One of these studies (Iacoboni et al. 1999) has shown that the mirror-neuron phenomenon is

---

2. In the sidebars that have quotes from the publication source, I have always put any words I added to the text in brackets but have not indicated elisions.

THE DISCOVERY OF MIRROR NEURONS

[While researching the action of motor neurons in macaques, the research team observed the following event that led to the discovery of mirror neurons.]

Scientific discoveries very often happen by chance: the discovery of mirror neurons makes no exception. One afternoon, when studying a neuron motorically activated by the action of grasping with the hand, one of us brought his hand toward a food-tray to grasp a raisin that had to be showed to the monkey: in that precise moment the neuron discharged vigorously. We were really surprised and, I must admit, quite skeptical about this unprecedented and unexpected visual response. Nevertheless, after many repetitions of the same action, we started thinking that a new class of visuo-motor neurons perhaps had been discovered. A class of neurons responding both when a particular action is performed by the recorded monkey and when the same action performed by another individual is observed. After that first neuron we decided to look systematically whether more grasping neurons could be activated not by the visual presentation of graspable objects but by the observation of grasping actions. I remember those days as marked by a growing sense of excitation as it appeared that a considerable percentage of grasping neurons could be driven by action observation. We decided to call them "Mirror neurons." Since then, many more mirror neurons have been recorded in our lab from many monkeys. This has allowed us to study them more quantitatively, and to theorize about their possible function.

Gallese 1999:3.

found in humans, where it involves Broca's area, as anticipated. This is strong support for the thesis that the vocalization of communication is associated with the purposeful use of arms and hands that are involved in making things.

I am not the first to see the relation between mirror neurons and speech. Vittorio Gallese (1999) has written that "the discovery of mirror neurons may provide a new, though still sketchy, neurobiological basis to account for the emergence of language." Those that have picked up on this have seen the relationship to gestures, as Giacomo Rizzolatti and Michael Arbib (1998) show in the title of their article, "Language Within Our Grasp," in which they relate mirror neurons to gesturing. V. S. Ramachandran (2002) says that mirror neurons might have brought about the so-called cultural explosion in the transition to the Upper Paleolithic, but certainly the emergence of language could not have been either so sudden or so late a human development.

Mirror neurons can best be thought of as a subset of motor neurons that serve to transfer specific bits of information from one individual to another and thus have a role to play in the learning process. It is too early to know just how extensive that role is, but if mirror neurons live up to their promise, they may serve as the *transfer of information between contemporaries* that is a rough counterpart to the role genes play for the transfer of information from one generation to another. The transfer of information from one living being to another is an essential quality of culture, distinguishing it from the biological transfer of information only from the living to the next generation. Finding the physical means by which information is shared with contemporaries is potentially of the greatest importance to culture theory; perhaps this is it.

Since this unique ability constitutes a veritable revolution, it had to be very closely tied to the basics of life, that is, directly associated with getting a livelihood. Since the fundamental strategy for making a living among humans is based on the use of the mind rather than on strength, these capabilities had to have such direct, pragmatic results. That is why I believe that the emergence of the logic of making things had to take place together with the logic of language. This belief seems so self-evident that I find it unimaginable that it is seen as heretical in the 21st century.

Our unleashed creative nature, in which both acts of making things and acts of talking are virtually infinite, is an end product of an evolution of the mammalian mind, a progression that starts with the genetically preprogrammed, yet locally adaptable, elaborate dams made by beavers responding sequentially to stimuli from water flow to the open-ended creation of a vaguely conceived chimpanzee sleeping nest and the more closely defined termite-fishing stick to the absolutely unlimited ability to create anything that can be realistically imagined for which the necessary materials are at hand. This seems also to be a progression in mental abilities in which the last stage has been achieved only by our own species. To achieve the fullness of culture, we must be able not only to make things, but also to talk about them.[3] It is worthwhile to note here in passing how different this evolution is to that of the birds, who emerged at about the same time and who also tend to their young. Bird nests also vary—much more than the lairs and nests of mammals—and some of them are far more elaborate than prehuman mammalian constructions, but they are species-specific and species-consistent. The same can be said for birdsong, suggesting a different cast of mind in avian evolution from that of mammalian.

To me, the most compelling reason to think that language evolved in tandem with making things is that it works by what I think of as "engineer's logic." It is a logic that has done wonders for our conquest of the world and it seems never to want for new frontiers—but it has its limitations. It is a logic that turns everything into entities and strings them into linear sequences, even things like time and space. There are aspects of the world of human beings that are not amenable to this treatment.

Let me digress on this topic, since it is intimately tied to the dynamics and limitations of human communication. Scientists have long recognized the limitations of linear logic and have developed statistical techniques to deal with them such as factor analysis. The latest iteration has been the formulation of mathematical models for what is known as "chaos" or "complexity" theory, in such diverse fields as physics, evolution, and economics. These are phenomena in the realms of "emergent" behavior, the transformation from one state to another, as in the origin of a new species or water changing into steam. They give mathematical solutions to

---

3. There is an unfortunate tendency, even among professionals, to proclaim that an animal "has culture" when it displays an intermediate and limited use of some cultural criterion, such as the traditions of termite fishing or the use of hammers and anvils to crack nuts. One attribute does not a culture make. Culture did not emerge full-blown out of Zeus's head. There are forms of behavior in local groups of other mammals that may be said to anticipate some aspect of culture. But if it means anything to say that a species "has culture," it must mean that it has systematic cultural motivation.

problems that have long been described in lay terms as context, a fundamental feature of ecological, and therefore also evolutionary, theory. Their studies have shown with mathematical precision that the iteration of behavior over time can result in a new state of equilibrium. Of interest here is that when the individual "actors" in such phenomena share a basic individual aim, the results seem foreordained—that is, they seem teleological. This seeming purposiveness in the realm of evolution is encapsulated in the phrase "the selfish gene," which, I have already noted, must have been the genetic trait that made the evolutionary process possible. In economics, it is the profit motive. Mitchell Waldrop (1992:146) speaks of this as an "implicit prediction," but it seems to me no more than a wish.

There are other problems with the way language handles the complexity of the world, especially in the formulation of categories. Dealing with smells is an example of an arena in which categorization is particularly difficult. Perhaps the sacrifice of olfaction on the altar of talking was a good trade because it is so hard to stuff smells into the Procrustean bed of three-dimensional space. Love is a second example of taxonomic difficulty, and this leads us to the next subject we must examine.

The Emotions

That older heritage that we call emotion does not, as I said, translate well into the reason-oriented world of speech. Emotions do not break down easily into the categories that discourse requires, nor do they respond to simple reasoning. To be sure, we manage to attach feeling to language with various literary devices and embellish it with gestures and intonation. Feeling and thinking are both processed in the brain and are interlinked; that is, thoughts evoke emotions and emotions influence thoughts. Their ancient purpose is to engage the person's urgent need to protect and to further his or her own interests by enhancing his responses and raising the level of his powers, whether for fight, flight, or sex. The evolutionary psychologists have emphasized the negative aspects of emotionality, seeing hostility as innate and the sex that is needed for procreation largely for its provocation to hostility in the service of the selfish gene. While there is no doubt that the human capacity for physical violence is a vital factor in social life and that it can be disruptive, this emphasis is misplaced. The aggressive life that hominids were to lead in order to take over diverse ecological niches could not be accomplished by animals with the emotional flaccidity of a manatee, popularly and appropriately called a sea-cow. The capacity for rage and the ability to transfer that sentiment into violent, destructive action had to be kept in the human animal. These emotions have been harnessed and directed to the welfare of the group. The issue therefore is not to condemn violence and other negative emotional behaviors per se, but to examine under what circumstances they get out of hand.

I shall limit my discussion to the sentiments attached to what we call love, arguably the most important word in our vocabulary. We love God and country, we love chocolate and rare steaks, we love our mothers and fathers, and we make love. There is a general common sentiment of good feeling or pleasure among all these and the other proper uses of the word love, but certainly the denotations vary widely. These extensions are of semantic interest; what is really important is the fact that there are two evolutionary sources of these sentiments that share the basic feature of strong, positive emotional attachment between two persons but that are in all other ways different. These are the feeling of sexual desire and the sense of physical gratification in nurturing and being nurtured. Sexual love and nurturant love not only have separate origins but also serve different purposes, and these purposes call for different attitudes and actions. We are so used to thinking of them as being alike that this separation of meaning can come as a shock. Indeed, we see romance as the basis for marriage, expecting the married couple to serve both these needs, "till death do us part." In most societies of the world, other considerations form the basis for conjugal life and reproduction, often with tacit recognition that some sexual desires will be satisfied elsewhere. In clan societies, rules of exogamy dominate the choice of spouse; in peasant societies the continuity of the farming enterprise regularly makes for a son bringing home the bride his parents have arranged for him. These confusions are confounded for us by the fact that much of the physical gratification in each activity is derived from the caressing that has a soothing effect, for in this there is behavioral overlap. It is imperative to take cognizance of their difference, for science cannot be the captive of folk concepts. Indeed, the conflation between the two meanings of love has been a source of much misunderstanding.

Sexual attraction is a very old attribute of life; it runs throughout the world's biota and has given both animals and plants some of their more inspired attributes. Sexual dichotomy requires that there be a relationship between two individuals of the same species, and this has affected both physical and behavioral attributes throughout the animal kingdom with a combination of attraction and hostility. It is inherently competitive, as the evolutionary biologists insist, for each individual seeks to do the mating in order to produce its own offspring in competition with all others of the same gender. A great deal of beauty along with a considerable amount of armament and nasty behavior have gone into the furtherance of this competition. Nothing in the human behavioral repertoire has received more anthropological attention than the ways the sexes relate to one another—sometimes with an almost prurient sense of delight. Though it is by no means a trivial subject, the emphasis is misplaced, for it is *not*, as Levi-Strauss said, the one place where nature and nurture meet.

That place can more accurately be assigned to nurturant love. Nurturant love is a more recent animal attribute, coming with the live births that are the hallmark of the mammal class of animals. Nurturance of birds is more limited, though it involves considerable parental care after the chicks are hatched. This was apparently foreshadowed by some dinosaurs. The inherent nature of nurturance is generosity. To nurture is to respond to a call to give one's time, energy, and resources to the welfare of another. To be truly nurturant is to take pleasure in giving such attention to the recipient because of a feeling of affection for him or her or for the sheer enjoyment of engaging in nurturant activity. This is not merely the "parental investment" that evolutionists call the time and energy that many animals, particularly insects, devote to protecting their progeny and securing their future. Insect investment is genetically programmed and does not involve direct association between genitor and progeny. The social insects do care for their larvae, but in ways that are more like an assembly line than human parenting. Mammals, on the other hand, regularly tend to their own infants and are programmed to enjoy it despite its many difficulties and unpleasantness.[4]

Freud, whose writings on love have been so influential, has conflated sexual and nurturant love—with unfortunate consequences. One consequence is the current tendency to disparage Freud for his mistakes rather than to correct them, throwing out the baby with the bathwater. His insight into the child's continued emotional involvement with parents, particularly the mother, is an important dynamic in the social life of humans everywhere. But, as we will see later, his explanation of this in terms of sexual love, as presented in his theory of the Oedipal complex, is simply a misrepresentation of the mother–child relationship. The real dynamic lies in the desire for the mother's nurturance: the sibling hostility coming from the competition for this vital gratification; the "womb envy" coming from the desire to return to these early comforts. Freud's recognition of the child's continuing wish for its mother's love was a major insight into human behavior, but his making it dependent upon libidinal desires was a major error— though an understandable one, in view of the general confusion about love. He also, it must be remembered, built his theories on the outpourings of troubled patients who often confused the two kinds of love and had delusional sexual fantasies about their parents. The child's eternal desire for the mother's approval is not sexual but the more mundane yearning for the comforts of infancy.

---

4. I was so appalled by the thought that the eminent ethologist who initiated sociobiology could disregard the social implications of the difference between insect and mammal reproductive systems that I wrote a novel (*The Valley of the Clones*) about a colony of cloned humans hidden in the Himalayas to show what a culture is like when the rank-and-file members are deprived of sex, reproduction, and the role of parenting. Unfortunately, the very point of the project proved to be so powerful that it destroyed the enterprise, as I had to turn my attention away from the clones to the colony of their keepers (not unlike colonial colonies everywhere) in order to get any conflict that could provide some drama.

The dynamics of this desire sets the tone for other social relations: toward the father who deflects the mother's attention and toward the siblings who took his place at her nurturing breast—ego deprivations rather than libidinal losses.

Both child and mother are programmed to seek and give expressions of affection; this is *the biological ontogeny of affect hunger*. Evolutionarily, it began as a device to assure the care and feeding of the neonate among social mammals and is built upon to motivate the neonate to learn from adults and thus to conform to the expectations of the troop, pride, or band and, finally, for human infants to undergo the lengthy curriculum necessary to become a human adult. This hunger for affection is essentially insatiable; it continues as a wish for acceptance, approval, and influence in the ever-expanding community in which every child is to live. It forms the source of those feelings of interdependence that are essential to social life and at the same time inspires the competitive quest for approval. In this it mimics the quest for sexual gratification. If the mother is loving and consistent, the child will want to follow the dictates she lays down. If she is an absent or unloving mother, the child will try to make up for the deprivation. ("Mother" here stands for all those who nurture the child, among whom she is normally paramount.) Freud's parable in *Totem and Taboo* (1909) of sons slaying their fathers relates to their desire for approval, not for access to maternal sex. If the father is supportive they want to demonstrate their worth to him; if he is negative they want to show him up. Since parents are rarely consistent in their behavior over the many years of the infant's dependency, the child's search for sense of self is far more complicated in reality than it is in the telling. This correction to Freud's Oedipal theories means that we should still recognize the dynamics of parent–child relations as a major force in cultural life but shifts its dramatic impact from the workings of the *id* to that of the *ego*. We return to this issue later.

The emotions that pit one person against another are an ancient heritage. Their usefulness to individual survival in the animal world is self-evident and their use for group protection is demonstrated by many ethological studies. Competition for mates is a major problem for all social mammals, exacerbated by the need to avoid inbreeding. Primate studies show diverse solutions, none of which seem to be part of the human heritage. We may take different views on this lack of clear precedent. On the one hand, we may argue whether some people are inherently more like chimps and others like bonobos or we can believe that we have eliminated all inherent predilections and left the matter entirely to cultural determination. Either way, these conflicting urges create a major problem for effective social life among humans. The solution to this problem was a cultural creation, not a genetic one, as in the case of language.

Ritual

If our present understanding of paleoanthropology is correct, the invention of ritual was a long time coming, for there is a long hiatus between the first appearance of fully modern humans making complicated spears and well-thought-out stone tools and the first evidence of ritual. But archaeology is fickle, changing its story with every new find, so we must be cautious as we try to make sense of what it is saying. Caution is particularly needed inasmuch as we have largely been watching the drama of early human prehistory on the European stage while the main events seem to have been taking place in Africa.

For some time we have been told that fully modern Homo sapiens existed at least 150,000 years ago, over a hundred millennia before the Upper Paleolithic began in Europe, some 40 thousand years ago. But we have already seen from Wynn's analysis of Isimilia's stone artifacts and from the spears found in a German mine that a sophisticated technical intelligence was at work that I (and paleoanthropologist Tobias) believe was associated with emerging linguistic capability. (A hundred millennia are but a blink in geological time, but an eternity in cultural time—in this instance, over twice, perhaps four times, as long as the remainder of human history.) Cultural growth sped up after the first evidences of ritual appear, often referred to as the "Upper Paleolithic cultural explosion." The gap is so widely known that the recent archaeological finds from Blombos Cave in Africa of pieces of hematite incised with some straight lines and of a cache of ordinary identically pierced seeds thought to have been beads, both dated at some 70 thousand years ago, became front-page news because they were seen as symbolic expressions 30 millennia before the European Upper Paleolithic began.

Why did it take a hundred thousand years for this change of evolutionary pace to happen? I suggest that the rational capacities for making things and for articulate language gave humans the material basis for population to increase but they still were unable to maintain the requisite social cohesion for the large societies they could create. (We return to this issue in a later chapter.) When we look at our present-day inability to make the moral adjustments needed to keep up with our technical innovations, it is not hard to think this was problematic at the dawn of humanity. Humans then could not invent *and agree to* social solutions to the demographic complexities that their technical innovations had made possible. It is not that moral philosophers were any less inventive than the artisans then (or now) but that social innovations were (and are) *less self-evidently* right than, for instance, the self-evident fact that a feathered arrow kept its course better than a bare one. It is not so easy to show that totemic beliefs make clans more effective, as in the case of the feathered arrow. The ends are not as clearly agreed upon in social devices nor are the causal relationships as monolithic with respect to social institutions like clans as they are with mechanical instruments. As I like to put it, "the guy being shot with the feathered arrow doesn't have a vote." Totemic beliefs were never discovered among the tribelets of central California, and these tribes were never strongly unified, though all the other features of clans were already in place, as I showed (1948) long ago. This lag time between what we accomplish in the technical sphere and what we accomplish in the social sphere is one reason a society is not always in sync with its ecology. We are no strangers to this phenomenon, for "social lag" has long been recognized as one of the problems inherent in our world of constant technological innovation. You may supply your own examples, but I like to point out that I am composing these words on a computer that has the old QWERT keyboard, developed to slow down the typist because the typewriter couldn't go fast enough, a practice that was already obsolete when I learned to type in high school. This example is amusing but trivial; a much more vital example is that modern technology has given us instantaneous global communication but we have not been able to establish the social devices to preserve global harmony.

Social devices are needed to create the emotional cohesion that makes for effective and continued collaboration and to reduce tensions between potentially hostile persons or groups. There are many ways in which the imaginative side of the human psyche is brought to bear on this problem, but I think that they come together in the creation of ritual. I consider ritual to be the second medium of communication and call it the language of sentiment. Rituals are a way to transfer feelings to others. They are not really language as I use the term because they do not employ grammar, syntax, or what I have called the engineer's logic, yet they clearly are a means of communication. They are group performances that induce the participants to act together for some social purposes or to make their new social roles public and to get others to accept the change. The former is exemplified by totemic rites and rituals of warfare, the latter by initiations and weddings, a distinction between what have come to be called rites of intensification and rites of passage, respectively. Unlike language, ritual does not require new physical or mental capacities and therefore does not call for further physical evolution. They hammer together and fine-tune existing responses to positive and negative experiences: The cacophony of fear, the drumbeat of excitement, the rhythms of the sex act, the soothing sounds of baby talk are all part of the repertoire of expressions and feelings already in place. So, too, with kinetic, visual, gustatory, and olfactory sensations. Add to these the normal pleasures of eating and sex, the effects of drugs and the displeasure of pain and you have all the raw materials needed for multimedia events that could make everybody involved feel the same way about whatever the group needs to feel about. If you want to psych up youths to go to battle, you get out the drums and gesticulate in unison (or, in our modern mechanized armies, pump heavy metal band music into our tanks to lessen the feeling of isolation and promote cohesion with buddies in other tanks as well as to drown out any humanizing cries from the enemy). If you want to solidify a group you eat together and sing and dance in unison to quite different rhythms. If you want to make youths recognize their responsibilities as adults and still keep them subordinate, you submit them to standardized indignities such as inflicted pain or enforced subordination that dramatize their new status and internalize its obligations. Rituals transmit feeling. This is so natural that it hardly needs saying. Rituals are given their cognitive meaning by being tied to beliefs through the use of speech. In this way, rites are related to existing, named social categories and statuses. Ritual communication stands in contrast to the engineer's logic of speech, supplementing it with what I call an "aesthetic appreciation" that transmits feelings from one person to another—not information about feeling, but the feeling itself. The aesthetic perception and the mechanical perception are two different ways of looking at reality, which is far more complex than either. The artist doesn't have to deny the reality of the entities within his painting, but his aim is to see the context in which its existence is important.

If, as I believe, rituals were fabricated out of the existing behavioral repertoire, they are the first major contribution humans made to their own condition—a cultural invention that made culture work. There is good reason to believe they are. The popular saying that "music is the universal language" implies as much, for the sounds out of which it is made are not strings of arbitrary phonemes but sounds that directly evoke certain feelings. These associations are basically a physiological response, though, as with all matters biological, they are also subject to cultural manipulation. While this is clearly the case with the quality and rhythms of sound, it seems likely to be the case with sight and other sensory stimuli. Watchmakers have found it necessary to set the watches in their advertisements at ten past ten, the shape of a smile!

Tools give the cultural mode of life its survival advantage, and language is the device that made culture possible, but ritual was needed to hold the social fabric together. The evidence for this is circumstantial but substantial: (1) The apparent long period of cultural stagnation in modern Homo sapiens before ritual appears; (2) the subsequent rapid growth of culture and the spread of people over the world, without any significant change in the human body; (3) the fact that rituals are made out of "raw materials" already in the repertoire of human behavior so that no further physical development was needed; (4) the rapid growth of culture once ritual is in place; and (5) the universality of ritual support for social institutions in tribal and modern communities. This thesis has the delicious appeal of irony: Finding imagination and sentiment are essential to the strength and power in a species that likes to think that the key to its superiority lies in intelligence and practicality.[5]

Psychological Miscellany

Someone who is going to string words together in order to convey a thought must have the mental apparatus to know about (be conscious of) the elements that go into that thought just as one that is going to shape raw materials into artifacts must be aware of the process to go through in getting there. We take consciousness for granted but there is no knowing how much it infuses animal life. We are ourselves not aware of much that our internal organs do or our senses record. We had to give up a lot of autonomic responses in order to achieve the awareness that the cultural life demands. Just giving up olfactory acuity of our ancestors was loss enough. A kind of blindness (called blindsight), which is not really blindness, dramatizes the difference. The eyes work normally and send cues to the brain but not to the *consciousness function* of the brain. The afflicted person's body-responses are appropriate even though he is unaware of what he has "seen." Ved Mehta, the insightful India-born memoirist writing for the *New Yorker,* who is proud of his ability to sense things without having sight and seems disdainful of the blind who can't, must have this kind of blindness. Is the cricket aware of its interest in finding a mate as it fills the night with its chirping? Is the bird thinking "property rights" as it sings? Is a vervet aware of snake-danger or even of snakes or of danger as a phenomenon when it gives its clever warnings?

---

5. To indulge in a personal note, the idea that religious belief trumps pragmatic knowledge is irony redux in being put forward by a scholar who is deeply troubled by the destructive force that belief has in the modern world.

Much of human memory, as well as the autonomous wiring of behavior remains outside of memory. This does not mean that these unconscious memories have no influence on behavior. Sohms and Turnbull (2002:279) say "Our every conscious moment is shaped by unconscious events, derived from a personal and biological past of which we have no inkling. 'Inherited' memories determine the *form* of the basic-emotion command systems." They go on to point out that those experiences that were sensed as good or bad are "the core of the system of implicit learning." If you daub a spot on a monkey's face and give it a mirror, it will take no note of the spot, but if you do that to a chimp, it will try to rub it off, suggesting that a level of self-awareness is found among apes that is not shared by monkeys. Culture depends on having self-awareness.

Consciousness, like learning, is not an unmixed blessing; it has great cost. It makes us aware of tragedy; it makes us able to remember our mistakes with the same intensity as we recall our triumphs. It gives us reason to fear our own future and makes us aware of the inevitability of our own death. Apes and elephants behave in ways that we read as grief over a death. Though they seem to grieve the loss, are they aware of their own death? Remarkable as the human ability to use logic is, the human ability to suppress and distort information is even more so. A great deal of culture is devoted to manipulating information and sentiments in the hope that people can face up to reality without being defeated by it. We seem to live with ambiguities, believing and disbelieving at the same time. Thomas Jefferson, who penned that great sentence saying that all men are created equal, owned slaves. Scientists often turn to God when they run out of explanations. This disingenuousness is not just a product of the Enlightenment. The linguist-anthropologist-psychiatrist Jaimie de Angulo trekked in the Ishi-country of northern California with a group of Indians in the early 1920s in Model-T Fords, and his report of how these "Stone-age Indians" used deductive logic and magical beliefs side by side offers us an example of the self-contradiction that characterizes so much human thought (see Sidebar 3). Nature is full of wonders, none more bizarre than the brain that can both remember and forget, both have faith and still doubt. We accommodate irrationality so as to tolerate the unthinkable.

EXPLAINING AND BELIEVING

We were going along the sagebrush, no road, just sagebrush, wind left, wind right, avoid this big clump, here's bad one, bump into the ditch . . . but there is no road at all anywhere, you are going through the brush, bumpety bump, all of us, six, seven, maybe eight cars, eight tin lizzies rattling through the sagebrush. Then, one morning, we had to stop. One of the tin lizzies was on the blink, and everybody got out to help. Then I witnessed something that amazed me. I had made up my mind that these men were straight out of the old Stone Age. I myself am not a mechanic; I hate machines; I am all thumbs; I don't understand machines; horses, yes; machines, no. And here I was watching these Stone Age men unscrew and rescrew and take things apart or out of the engine and spread them on a piece of canvas on the ground . . . but the amazing thing to me was their argumentation. It was perfectly logical. ". . . It can't be the ignition, look, I get a spark . . . I tell you, it's in the transmission . . . Now pull that lever . . ." Maybe I was over-impressed because the simplest machine smells of magic to me. Maybe I missed a lot of their argument because off and on they would lapse into Pit River. They called the battery *hadatsi*, "heart"; a wheel is *pi'nine* (a hoop used in the old days for target practice); and so on and so forth. But certainly they made use of logic just as any white man would. Finally the engine, or whatever was wrong, was repaired. Then I overheard one young fellow say to another: "You know why this happened? Because he has been sleeping with his woman while she was menstruating! That's against the rules."

Angulo 1990:55–56.

Another manifestation of the human psyche is the ability to make firm psychological attachments to things, people, and concepts—Freud's "cathexis." The idea that people and things are interchangeable is an essential ingredient in our society and economy and is widely, if not universally, incorporated into social life. In tribal societies it may be a spiritual matter; among us it is a legal fiction, but these are just cultural definitions of universal sentiments. The number of human lives that were saved by the invention of *wergild*, the payment in "valuables" instead of exacting blood revenge (substituting things for kinsmen to be killed), is unknowable, but it must have been large. The exchange of objects for wives was a cultural innovation that made trading sisters easier, if no less dishonorable. Tokens given value made it possible to engage in trade, and trade was increasingly necessary for getting the diverse raw materials that advancing technology required.

Things are not just things in tribal societies any more than they are in modern industrial societies. Possessions are universally endowed with meaningfulness; identification with the object has a mystical, magical quality. Many of the things that play this role are associated with religious belief and ritual, but ownership of secular goods can have just as strong a psychological involvement. Let some examples show what I mean. The Hupa, among whom property is unusually fraught with meaning, use dugout canoes. When a man needs to cross the river he may use any he finds tied up at the riverbank. Should it capsize and he drown, his family may sue the owner on the grounds that such an accident came from the "subliminal wish" of the owner, as we would say. In a psychological sense, the Hupa see the boat as an extension of the person. Though we do not subscribe to such psychic powers, our sense of identification with property still can hold an owner liable in a court of law. The psychic importance of objects is indicated as early as the Upper Paleolithic. When I visited Les Eysies, Hallam Movius showed me a Lower Paleolithic hand axe that came from an Upper Paleolithic deposit. The thought that these Cro Magnon people had brought this exotic object back to camp and preserved it seems to me to be an early example of vesting objects with special meaning. Did they endow them with the special power of "thunder stones" as European peasants, New Guinea tribesmen, and East Texas farmers do?

The Aranda of Australia travel naked over their desert territory carrying only their basic necessities: spear and spear thrower, digging stick, a shallow wooden vessel on the women's heads, and perhaps a girdle made of the hair of an ancestor, imbued with the magic powers of that deceased relative. But they keep in a sacred and secret cache hidden from the eyes of women and the uninitiated men the *churingas* that embody their soul or the souls of ancestors. These oblong stone or wooden icons are engraved with cabalistic symbols and treated with great reverence. A film taken in the 1930s of old men opening the cache and chanting and rubbing these icons with fat and ochre remains in my memory as a deeply felt and touching display of religious devotion. (The film is no longer shown, honoring the request of the Aranda.) These sacred objects, embodying the souls of their living and dead clansmen, were loaned to other clans during disputes to serve as hostages, letting the spirits of the dead take the place of the living. The San of the Kalahari Desert seem not to have any such objects of personal identification, which was the point of the cult film *The Gods Must Be Crazy*. Yet the psychology is not alien to native San sentiment, as shown by the refusal of a gift offered by an anthropologist to a local leader, who said he did not want to feel the envy of others.

The human brain is a constant source of wonderment. We are just beginning to explore its mysteries and most of us haven't even formulated the questions we should put to it, if we could. The human animal has to forget as well as remember, to compartmentalize the world and still see its interconnectedness, to explain away as well as explain the existential tragedies. It involves a delicate balance of opposites, like a thermostatic device with near-zero tolerance. I am sure I have here only touched the surface of the issues that had to be solved before the human kind of life could be sustained. Indeed, in this way of perceiving the human condition, the shift to humanity involved the creation of a mythical reality, a perception of the universe and our place in it that made the tragedies inherent in human existence tolerable. And this mythic reality had to be felt and seen; it was the purely human invention of ritual that was the capstone.

4

Affect Hunger

Affect hunger is the motivating force for sociality, just as thirst motivates us to drink and hunger to eat. In this chapter we examine the details of how it works. We first look at the tools that human infants inherit to transfer this yen for response into action and to elicit the desired responses from their caretakers. We can then look at some of the chemistry involved and the neurons that fire to convey the information. The details of such matters are far from clear, but we know enough to appreciate what is going on.

Definition

The human infant is born with a need that I have called affect hunger. Affect hunger is the urge to get expressions of affection from others. It has its biological basis in the imperative need for tactile stimuli. Such stimuli are necessary for the newborn child, pup, or kitten to have a normal growth of dendrites and a full complement of synapses on its nerve cells. It is not an exaggeration to say that these stimuli are as requisite to normal health as food itself. Kittens and puppies must be licked and monkey infants groomed by their mothers in order for these features of the central nervous system to develop. What we see as hygiene is not merely done for cleanliness but also to make the nerve cells grow properly. The famous Harlow studies (1959) of Rhesus monkeys showed that infants deprived of tactile stimulation developed psychotic behavior and did not grow into normal monkeys. Psychiatrist René Spitz (1965) had earlier found similar physical and behavioral problems among children raised in orphanages where all the physical needs were met but where the children were given no affectionate attention. We are therefore talking about hunger in the fundamental meaning of the word—a built-in urge that induces the individual to meet a physical need that is essential for a healthy body. At the outset this must be supplied by the mothers. Human mothers replace licking and grooming with cuddling and caressing. The evolutionary process made it mandatory for mothers to do this if they wanted healthy children. The Harlow experiments were dramatic evidence of the effect of affect starvation on the monkeys' psyches and they also demonstrated the two-way interaction between social experience and social performance. Harlow had artificially impregnated females who had been raised under his regime of affect deprivation and so had had no infantile experience of affect. He found that such mothers rejected their own newborns. However, some of the more persistent infants managed to gain some physical response from the mother and in so doing triggered a latent predilection for mothering in these affectless mothers who, as time went on, became increasingly maternal (see Sidebar 4). Think about this. Something inherent in the mother survived her own lack of those experiences that are supposed to trigger affection and can, with much greater difficulty, be awakened by the persistent affective demands of another!

The Ethology of Infancy

Viviparous birth calls for mothers who are programmed to sacrifice time, energy, and freedom for the welfare of their progeny. There are dozens if not hundreds of specific inherited traits of behavior that go into making successful mothers and successful infants. The difficulties involved are not always overcome, as mortality rates among primates of all kinds indicate. Sarah Hrdy (1999) has shown us that many problems can arise from uncommitted caretakers or lapses in the infant's charms. Child development specialists have shown that infants are programmed to seek

SOCIAL INDUCEMENT TO MOTHERING

[We studied female monkeys that were] subjected to early social isolation. They had reached sexual maturity but were apathetic or adamantly uncooperative when confronted with breeding-stock males that were sexually eager and adroit. By methods dark, dismal, and devious we impregnated several of these reluctant females over a period of years. We have called them "motherless mothers," since they never experienced mother love, nor any other kind of monkey affection, themselves. Most of the motherless mothers either completely ignored or abused their initial offspring. . . . However, unless the mothers actually killed their infants—and several did—the babies struggled for maternal contact day after day, week after week, month after month. The infants would cling to the mothers' backs, continually attempting to achieve ventral and breast contact despite efforts by the mothers to displace them. To our surprise, maternal brutality and indifference gradually decreased. From the fourth month onward, the persistent babies that were finally able to attain intimate physical contact with their mother were actually punished less and permitted nipple contact more than offspring of normal mothers.

Many of the motherless mothers have had second and even third babies. Those whose maternal feelings were eventually released by the persistent and determined body contact and nursing efforts of their first infants proved to be adequate or good mothers to their subsequent babies. Most of the motherless mothers that had abused or ignored their first infants throughout a predetermined 6-month postpartum period continued to be inadequate, brutal, or lethal mothers to subsequent progeny.

It seems that in the case of the adequate mothers, the babies inadvertently served as psychotherapists to their indifferent mothers and that these mothers spontaneously transferred maternal feelings induced by their first babies to their feelings for subsequent babies. The data on the rehabilitated mothers suggested that infants possess some specific abilities as behavioral therapists for abnormal adult females. However, rehabilitation was limited to maternal behavior and, in particular, those mothers continued to exhibit inappropriate and ineffective sexual behavior.

Harlow 1959:297.

affective responses as well as food. Affect often seems to have priority over food in the infant's scale of desires. To achieve these ends, human infants have what I call "sociophilic traits" that constitute the ethology of infancy. It is a constant wonder to me that the biology-minded anthropologists and human evolutionists seem not to be aware of them. We will examine a few.

The infant comes with some instinctive behavior such as the nuzzling-suckling response. As surely as a puppy or kitten, a baby will seek the mother's nipple and start to suck. It also retains the grasping instinct that had originally been essential to monkey infancy. Babies are born with the ability to communicate discomfort and in a few weeks can show pleasure through that most ingratiating of all acts, smiling. (Why should smiling be ingratiating? Why do smiles make us feel good? Adults are also programmed to respond to a baby's cues. Both parties have a biological basis to their communication.)

Colwyn Trevarthen, a leading figure in this research summarizing the study of early infancy (1979), says that the human infant is intentional, conscious, and personal. He emphasizes the inherent faculty for intersubjectivity, involving an awareness of other persons, negotiation of relationships with others, and evoking others' responses. Intersubjectivity is an ability that rapidly grows and takes control over the infant's experiences and soon becomes the central motivator and regulator of mental growth.

The human face plays a most significant role in sociality. There is an area of the brain specifically devoted to facial recognition (Geschwind 1979). Spitz had early noted that infants will track only on a human face and at birth will already track on patterns that have facelike properties (Johnson et al. 1991).

Imitation is essential to culture. Research by Andrew Meltzoff and M. Keith Moore (1977) established that babies two or three weeks old can imitate such facial expressions as protruding the lip, opening the mouth, and sticking out the tongue. More recent research has found three-day-old babies aping expressions.

Learning is an inherited capacity that is immediately brought into play by the neonate. Hanus and Mechthild Papousek (1979) showed that infants are capable of learning during the first week of life (though not as fast as they will at three months). This learning has an affective component, for signs of pleasure appear when babies get the desired response, and signs of displeasure appear at unsatisfactory ones. The Papouseks have also demonstrated that a dialogue goes on between the infant and its mother, each being alert to the other's signals. Frame-by-frame videos of such mother–child interaction show that the mother responds to the needs of the infant in consistent ways with simple, repetitious vocalizations, special facial expressions, and body movements. "Dialogue" is not just a figure of speech but has real validity, for the communication that goes on is behaviorally like conversation though the subject matter of the discourse is emotional rather than informational and is conveyed by sound quality and tactile signals rather than words. Conditioning is happening; education has begun. The infant expresses doubt, surprise, annoyance, denial, agreement, enjoyment, and affirmation. There is turn-taking and synchronized movement between them as in adult conversation. This is so spontaneous that even the mother is not aware that she is doing these things. Such discourse is not just full of pleasantries, but may express annoyance and negation from either or both sides. The infant is acquiring a large body of information about local proprieties in these early encounters with the adult world and is being motivated to behave the way the adults want it to even before there is any explicit content— only affect.

The urgency of this inherent dialogue lies at the base of a phenomenon that psychiatrist John Bowlby (1982) called "attachment." Attachment is not just bonding, though perhaps it is built upon it, for it is far more complex and emotion laden. Humans do bond; the neonate immediately responds to the mother's voice, a counterpart to the gosling's visual bonding. Bonding is passive behavior while attachment is the active pursuit of mutuality. This is what was at stake among Spitz's unloved orphans and Harlow's wire mother–raised monkeys. Bowlby had been influenced by these studies.

As with so much in the realm of evolution, Darwin was the first to call attention to the use of gesture in communicating emotions. In *The Expression of the Emotions in Man and Animals* (1872) he noted that body movements and facial expression serve as the first means of communication between the mother and infant. Bowlby pointed out that these were value laden, Westen (1997) says that their driving motive is to regulate affect (minimizing unpleasant and maximizing pleasant feelings), and Feldman and Greenbaum (1997) have noted that this regulation of emotions operates outside awareness.

Attachment appears to be part of the infant's search for a secure haven, for the certainty that somebody will take care of it, giving it the cuddling its psyche needs along with the food and warmth its body needs. At the outset the baby looks to anyone in its social surroundings for such support but soon focuses on one familiar individual—normally the mother. By the twelfth week it is responding to this mother-figure differently than it responds to others. The essential content of those dialogues are the request for this nurturant love and the assurance that it will be given. All those infant tricks to induce parental response and love are in the service of making a secure and satisfying attachment. The triggering mechanism for this search for attachment is, of course, the hunger for affective response.

The success of these tricks varies. Mothers vary in their commitment to and talent for motherhood, circumstances vary in giving support to the relationship, and, finally, the infant brings its own talents and disabilities to the dialogue. Babies are different in temperament.[1] Some are more sensitive, irritable, responsive, or phlegmatic than others and a mother's behavior is affected by the specifics of her infant's predisposition. The optimal nurturant relationship is that each party to it both gives and receives gratification from it, just as is the case with what is optimal in sexual intercourse.

The success of these encounters matters. Sarah Hrdy was originally drawn to primate studies to solve, among other things, the enigma of primate infanticide, and she discovered that a passive (and sometimes active) parental involvement in an infant's deaths is not rare in the animal kingdom—or in the more recent history

---

1. I beg the question whether such early variation is genetic or situationally determined but suspect they are both, as many nongenetic factors, such as intrauterine chemicals, can be involved.

of humanity. She is far too wise to justify this as the workings of "the selfish gene," though she is aware of animal instincts that propel such behavior. It is a morality tale. What is important to us, however, is that she illuminates (1999) the pressure on infants to elicit the maternal affection (which the mother is preprogrammed to perform) in a chapter appropriately called "Why Be Adorable?" Hrdy supports her argument that these wiles are imperative for the child's survival by recording instances in which failure to do so has led to the infant's death.

Mary Ainsworth (1967) initiated her research on attachment in Uganda where, as it happened, I met her. She was too early in her studies and I still too naive in my understanding of the subject for me to anticipate the impact her work would have on the under-standing of child development. She was finding a way to mea-sure the urge for attachment and in the process saw the psycho-logical result of flawed ones. The research protocol that ultimately she established is basically simple: a scripted departure by the mother and the observation of the infant's behavior when the mother departed, during her absence, and upon her return. A se-cure infant handles this situation without difficulty but the inse-curely attached child shows distress at her absence and clings tightly to her when she returns. Very insecure infants, whether monkey or human, suffer deep psychological trauma. A good attachment gives a child a sense of security and feeling of com-petence that affects his performance throughout life while the traumas of insecure attachments will have negative effects on the adult's personality. These findings are very useful to child psy-chologists, but our interest is more theoretical: the evidence that affect hunger is indeed a universal imperative human urge. But what makes for a *good adjustment* is another matter. Attachment is thus a basic process in infant development; what constitutes a *good* attachment is a cultural matter—a value judgment. Tom Weisner (1996) makes this case with the comments of a mother who was pleased with her son's response to this test, though the child was scored as a problematic "avoidant" by the testing team. She exulted: "This is what I have been working for by having him be with other kids and families while I am working. Look how independent he is. See how he can play by himself?" (313).

All these events of the early months of life are stored in memories and affect a person's attitudes and moods throughout life, even though they cannot be called to consciousness. Brain research specialists say this material is stored as "intrinsic memory," as distinct from what is available for our conscious use, which they call "extrinsic memory." (If I had had standing in this fraternity of brain researchers, I would have urged that they be called "covert" and "overt," for they seem to differ not so much in how the memory is stored as in the mode of its retrieval.) Extrinsic memory is largely retrieved with verbal ties and other associated events that are not available to the newborn infants who have only the relatively inchoate sensory associations for bringing these early memories into consciousness. Whatever we call them, these early memories are lodged in our brains and affect our outlook for the rest of our lives. Intrinsic memory appears to be the physical reality of Freud's "unconscious." Solms and Turnbull (2002)[2] point out "that the memories we do encode during the very early years will take the form of habits and beliefs . . . rather than explicit, episodic memories." They go on to say that they "have every reason to expect that early experience has a decisive impact on personality development . . . but [that] it seems highly unlikely that anyone can explicitly remember any event that happened to them in the first 18–24 months of life." (169)

The Chemistry of Affect Hunger

The physical manifestations of all that is going on is complex and I can give only some basic facts on the role of peptides in social interaction. The neuropeptides, oxytocin and vasopressin, unique

---

2. Had I had *The Brain and the Inner World* at the outset, writing this book would have been much easier. Learning of it only as I was correcting proofs made me aware of the new intellectual movement called neuropsychoanalysis, which bridges the gap between neurobiology's study of the brain and psychoanalysis's examination of the mind. Anybody tackling the issue addressed in my book must be aware of this body of work. When I picked it up, it was with some trepidation, but I have found no areas of disagreement. Here and elsewhere I am using it for illumination and corroboration.

to mammals, are closely associated with initiating nurturance in the female and in bonding with infants (and in other relationships). Mothering behavior varies widely in intensity among mammals. Some shrews and rabbits spend but a few minutes each day with their young, while among other species (including some primates) some mothers are "promiscuously parental," that is, will even be parental to the young of other mothers. The peptides that affect acceptance and rejection of others tend to perform only under specific environmental stimuli. The neuropeptides (prolactin and oxytocin) that are involved in lactation are also implicated as mediators of maternal care. There seem to be ecologically significant ways in which these neuropeptides express themselves in different species of animals. Ewes, which have only the passive sociality of herd life, make bonds with their own lamb by smell immediately after delivery and reject all other lambs. Pregnant female Norway rats will avoid or attack pups they see during early pregnancy but just before delivery will start to do nurturant things like nest-building and will even retrieve and defend other mothers' pups. Apparently the triggering action varies from species to species and perhaps from one situation to another. My purpose in this description is not to give a lesson in the chemistry of affect expression but only to show that there is such a chemistry. We see in this that chemical action in the neurological activity for expressions of affect works differently from one species to another, that the way it works can also be situation-dependent, and that such determinative situations can be induced by social interaction. These are fundamental observations in support of my thesis of the dynamic interaction between biology and culture.

In the cautious language of science, Insel and Young (see Sidebar 5) suggest that these chemicals are the same ones that serve as the inducements that make for drug addiction. Apparently the chemicals fire some hedonistic neurons like the ones that James Olds uncovered in his research. Olds put rats on a maze that led to food, but a stimulus along the way fired on neurons that gave the rats such gratification that they stopped then and there to take hit after hit rather than go on to get the food they had been after. What Freud called "the pleasure principle" is not just a social

THE CHEMISTRY OF CARING

Attachment behaviour is both biologically important and technically difficult to study. The behaviour is complex and there are changes in several cognitive and affective variables to consider. Nevertheless, recent studies with chicks, rats, sheep, voles and now humans have begun to reveal some important candidates for the neurobiology of social attachment. The neuropeptides oxytocin and vasopressin have yielded a model that links molecular, cellular and systems approaches. Dopamine pathways in the forebrain, especially the nucleus accumbens and ventral palidum, seem important for certain aspects of partner preference formation. It seems likely that for attachment to occur, these neuropeptides must link social stimuli to dopamine pathways associated with reinforcement. It is also possible that neural mechanisms that we associate with drug abuse and addiction might have evolved for social recognition, reward and euphoria—critical elements in the process of attachment. In the very near future, we can hope that discoveries of the molecular and cellular mechanisms of addiction might be applied to the neurobiology of attachment, providing a new understanding of one of our most complex and intriguing emotions.

A recent functional resonance imaging (fMRI) study of adult [humans] looking at pictures of their partner as opposed to close non-romantic friends [found the] pattern of cortical activation was distinct from previous studies of face recognition, visual attention, sexual arousal or other emotional states, but resembled preliminary results from an fMRI study of new mothers listening to infant cries. Both studies of human attachment show marked overlap between the pattern of activation when looking or hearing a loved one and a previous report of activation during cocaine-induced euphoria. It seems likely that pathways that mediate the hedonic properties of psychostimulants evolved as neural systems for social attachment.

Insel and Young 2001:134.

construct but a concrete physical reality. The implication is clear that the evolutionary process had to give mothers strong motivation to keep them at the inherently irksome tasks of mothering. I am indebted to Insel and Young, who summarized the evidence for the chemistry of attachment in animals and humans for us.

One may reasonably wonder if in some way the experiences of the affectless mothers in Harlow's experiment (see Sidebar 4) might not have induced such chemicals in their neurological systems.

The Brain and Affect Hunger

Current brain research is beginning to pry open the black box that holds the hardware connecting the stimuli to the impulses and actions that result in what we do, think, and feel. From my perspective, the most important thing that this research tells us is that the brain is a malleable organ that is constantly being shaped and reshaped by the stimuli it experiences. I do not mean simply that our thoughts are affected by our experiences, but that *the physical structure of the brain itself is changed.* I start with the view that the mind is the activity that the brain engages in, but we find it hard to think of the activity shaping the structure.[3] But that is what is happening. This should not be so surprising when we remember that exercise shapes our body. The idea that the brain is like a vessel to be filled is hard to discard. While there is much still to learn about the brain, enough is known to support the thesis of behavioral malleability and social interaction as one source of stimulation of such change.

The human brain is not fully developed nor are its functions fully organized at birth. This is not merely because they do not have all of the needed synapses and dendrites, as I have already noted, but because the new ones that come into being in response to the infant's social experiences and activities are establishing new brain functions. These experiences include the dialogue between child and mother, already discussed, which do not merely add to the child's store of memory but affect the brain's structure. The part of the brain involved at the outset is the right hemisphere, which processes voice tone, gestures, and facial expressions signaling the mother's sentiments (Siegel 2001). This, as Freud anticipated with

---

3. We should think of "mind" as really being the verb "minding," as digesting is what the digestion tract does, for then we would have less trouble understanding this.

the concept of the subconscious, is the bedrock of every child's intrinsic memory. The stimulus and responses here are so "natural" that one does not think to look for a mechanism in the brain to effect the transmission of the mother's signals to the infant's brain. Current brain research has, however, found such an instrument: the mirror neurons that we discussed earlier to show their apparent role in the transmission of language.

The studies that I have cited show the two-way flow of energy and information between the realms of cultural and physical realities. These examples run against the presumed flow of causation that lies deep in Western thought, namely, that the "hard" matter of physical things causes change in the "intangibles" of behavior and thought. This gives these findings a special poignancy that goes beyond the consideration of affect hunger and has important implications for culture itself—and even, I suggest, for scientific theory. Thought influences not only behavior but also physiology and physique. This we already knew in an anecdotal way from the ethnographic literature on sorcery and trance; it expands our notions of the possible. The biological program that serves the baby's entrance into the world is humanity's most important genetic heritage. In contrast to received wisdom that sees sex as the place where biology and culture meet, it is in the parturition and nursing where the transfer takes place. This thesis, and the biological knowledge that it incorporates, has profound epistemological implications, for it is a denial of the separate spheres of knowledge that are part of scholarly presuppositions.

Affect Hunger and the Social Order

Affect hunger can only be gratified by others; it is therefore immediately implicated in the existence and nature of social relations. It is gratified in many different specific ways, but there are two general ways to meet this need: belonging and performance. Belonging involves a sense of oneness with others in the environment, and this, of course, means some defined and identified community of people. Performance means ability and proficiency in doing things that the individual feels is worthwhile. That belonging involves others is self-evident, but performance is ego-gratifying to the extent that it is seen to conform to some public perception of what is useful or good. What kinds of groups exist and what kinds of performance meet the criteria of the good and the useful vary from one culture to another. They vary both in self-evident ways and in obscure, covert ways. We look next at the way the infant acquires these cultural directives, then at how this translates into culture, and later at the role and fate of affect gratification as they change under differing ecological circumstances as a result of cultural evolution.

5

Revolution in the Nursery

We are now prepared to put together the story of one of the climactic events in the history of all living matter. It opened up a new way of life, no less innovative in making new lifestyles available than was the first vertebrates' move onto land or the acquisition of internal temperature control. This revolution was to override the basic premise on which evolution is built—that every change in inherited physical features or hard-wired behavior must improve the chances for survival of offspring. Ironically, by overriding that sacred evolutionary principle this event created a being with extraordinary survival capacity. This revolution took place in the nursery; more accurately, it reiteratively has taken place in every nursery since humanity came on earth.

Summary of Our Heritage

Let us review what the evolutionary process had brought to these nurseries: a body standing upright with ease; hands capable of varied and intricate manipulations ranging from throwing heavy objects to fingering a violin (preprogrammed only for the grasping reflex); blood flowing through the body that maintains internal climate control; a digestive system able to process a wide variety of foods; a nervous system programmed for flexibility, giving wiggle-room for learning; a brain with a built-in program for the logic of grammar and the reasoning needed to make things and a

mechanism for learning from others how to do things; the ability
to bring perceptions (including perceptions of the self) into consciousness; a hunger for affective responses that induces infants to
actively seek the social intercourse necessary for the learning they
must undergo; a host of behavioral traits designed to elicit favorable responses from others and to discourage unfavorable ones;
and (later, as adults) the ability to read and respond appropriately
to such blandishments and find psychological rewards for spend-
ing the time and energy in the parental role. Finally, these infants
are born long before they are able to fend for themselves, giving
them the many years needed to learn the complicated system of
communication by means of which their parents could picture the
world in which they were to live the rest of their lives and the
rules under which they were to live. Some of these features are
found in embryonic form among our primate ancestry but they
are *all* inherent in Homo sapiens.

The Nature of the Revolution

This nursery revolution removed us from the family and genus of
our primate forebears into a unique species that rejects the autoc-
racy of the ancient demand for genetic continuity in favor of actions serving other aims. It enabled adults to inculcate in their
young the motive to do the things those parents want them to do,
even when they flouted evolutionary principles. The adults involved in this recurrent nursery drama had already undergone
this initiation and thus are just passing on standardized (i.e., cultural) expectations. They don't see it this way; in their minds they
are just trying to take care of the beings they find themselves
charged with, to minimize the aggravations and maximize the rewards that go with the job. Sometimes they are consciously teaching what they know, but often, especially at the outset, they are
just doing "what comes naturally"—though what they do is in
fact highly affected by their culture. The result is to transform the
neonate into a responsible and competent member of his or her
society. In the long, intimate affective "conversations" that take
place between infant and caretaker, the child gradually acquires
the subtle qualities of character and behavior of that culture by

learning what evokes the affective responses it is seeking and what wards off painful rejections.

It is not coincidental that these cultural motives are inculcated before the hormones that provoke sexual desire have kicked in. The chemical changes at puberty raise in growing children the urges that trigger their own need for self-definition. One might say that every child is an unwitting signatory to a social contract to behave according to local custom and only gets to read the fine print at adolescence. That is why adolescence is often so stormy and why so many cultures include rituals that reassert the demands of the social order. In this long apprenticeship the child acquires some indefinable something that stands in the place of his biological being, an imaginary self that lives in the imaginary world of culture.

"Intrinsic" Indoctrination of Personality

There undoubtedly are many factors that enter into the formulation of each person's individual "personality," and important among them are the experiences of early infancy. I believe that the affective content of the parent–child dialogues are among the most significant sources in forming these characterological features, being laid down in the intrinsic memory of infants before they understand speech. These are the deeply felt but unverbalized feelings about the self and others, the qualities that enter into popular stereotypes of peoples and therefore are among the more subtle aspects of culture: the emotional volatility of the Italians, the emotional restraint of the British, the *Ordentlichkeit* of the Germans. Such stereotypic forms of behavior were thought to be "racial" and were often exaggerated and used to denigrate other cultures in the expression of xenophobic prejudice. These are real differences in behavioral tendencies, but they are not racial. They are, rather, deep-seated behavioral expectations that are transmitted from parent to child in those wordless dialogues between mother and infant.

A recent experiment gives explicit support for the psychological and social importance of this early mother–child dialogue. The authors compared the early child-rearing practices of the agricultural Nso and the pastoral Fulani who live in Cameroon (Yovsi and Keller 2003).[1] They describe differences in both practice and belief: The settled Nso farmers reinforce mutuality by strengthening mother–infant ties and shared care-giving among kindred women and display social warmth by a generous feeding regime; the pastoral Fulani reinforce independence by the isolation of the mother–child dyad, by suppressing expressions of affect, and by a less indulgent feeding regime, preparing the infant for a more stoic adult life. The authors' descriptive data are given in Sidebar 6, but they also made observational data on samples of mother–child dyads from each group and found statistically significant behavioral differences with respect to affective relationships on five measures that induce or express social warmth. These included the two measures of interaction between mother and child, one involving tactile behavior and the other facial expressions, as well as holding the child closely, maternal gazing at the child, and tactile stimulation. These were all interactive behaviors of care-takers; none of the babies' own actions varied significantly. This shows that the infants are born with the same impulses and that it is the adult behavior that brings on later behavior.

This study of child-rearing brings me back to earlier studies of the ethnography of infancy. In the late twenties and until after World War II, research was designed to show that those subtle but inescapable differences among the people of Europe that were popularly thought of as racial could better be seen as cultural. Researchers therefore studied similar kinds of variation among the cultures of different tribal peoples and built up a large and interesting corpus of data on child-rearing in tribal societies. Taking inspiration from Freudian ideas of sexual development, many

---

1. It is not entirely coincidental that this is the same contrast that I studied in East Africa (see later), since the difference in the career demands between pastoralism and farming is the most dramatic to be found among tribal economies. I was not prepared to make such an investigation but have long wanted to sponsor such research, for I think this may have relevance to the differences among ethnic minorities in their adaptation to our society.

NEONATE CULTURAL INDOCTRINATION

Nso Farmers

When a child is born to a [Nso farming] family, the mother puts the child to the breast immediately since it is believed the baby should have contact with her and the mother's breast before swallowing anything else. The mother is assisted not only by women from her lineage but also by anyone who feels he or she can contribute to the well-being of the mother and infant. Breastfeeding is one of the areas in which the mother is helped with nutritious food items or made to drink fresh palm wine to enable a sufficient flow of breast milk for the child. Breasts are believed to be only for infant feeding. Breast milk is considered to be the only food that can make the child grow healthy, and breasts are not seen as erotic objects. At times the mother and child are secluded in order for the mother to concentrate on the care of her child, protect the child from witches.

There are Nso beliefs that could be seen as probreast-feeding theories. When the mother is away from her baby and the breast milk starts flowing, it is believed the child is hungry, crying, or uncomfortable, and this should make the mother hurry to breastfeed her baby. Breast milk is thought to have medicinal effects, so it is dropped into the child's eyes and ears or in a newly circumcised baby's penis to heal infections or wounds. If the child gets hurt, milk is also used to calm down the pains and make the child feel comfortable. Breastfeeding, according to the Nso, satisfies the child and brings him and the mother in close contact in order for him to feel her body and grow well. It is believed that breastfed children seldom cry. Breastfeeding is also believed to relieve the mother and make her feel comfortable as well as help her accomplish her duties of motherhood.

Fulani Pastoralists

With the Fulani, childbirth is a private event since it is the result of a sexual activity. It is usually hidden, as the pregnant woman is secluded in her hut or leaves her parents' homestead. She conceals the pregnancy by covering her head and the protruding stomach with a wrapper. During birth, the woman delivers alone. This is especially true with the birth of the first child, and it is only when the child cries that other women can come to assist. Immediately after birth, the mother and the child will have no contact, as the grandmother cares for the child while the mother is resting. The Fulani tend to give water immediately after delivery because they believe that water clears the throat of the newborn, which is good for his health. The Fulani believe that colostrum is not good for the child, and the child stays for hours or days without the taste of the breast milk. During this period, he is given just water. The Fulani believe that the breast milk should be clean and white like cow milk before it can be given to the child since whiteness is customarily associated with purity. [They] avoid exposing their bodies publicly but breastfeed in a confined place. Breast milk is considered to be the infant's food for about two years. A Fulani man could even divorce his wife if she did not breastfeed the child for the mandated period. This is due to the Fulani belief that only children who were not fully breastfed can lose their herd or mismanage them and tend to depend on others for a living.

In Fulani society, eye contact is forbidden between children and their elders, especially parents, because it is believed to create an intimacy that should not exist in a parent-child relationship. Hugging or holding is prohibited among the Fulani, and seen as an erotic gesture reserved only for sexual partners. It is believed that when the woman is happy and shows interest in the child, the evil eye can curse or kill the child.

Yovsi and Keller 2003:150–154.

anthropologists looked for the answer in the way babies were handled. Freud's theory of psychosocial development focused on the traumas of infancy and childhood, postulating a natural progression from oral to anal to genital eroticism during which attitudes were formed by conflicts over toilet training and weaning. The spate of studies dealing with the treatment of babies in different cultures gave no support for this Freudian thesis. At some time in the fifties, aware of this paradigm failure, this line of research was abandoned—a case of abandoning the enquiry rather than changing the paradigm. Nevertheless, a rich deposit of ethnographic data on the way different people treat their children and its relationship to their respective culture is available and we can now explore it in the light of an altered paradigm.

Gregory Bateson and Margaret Mead (1942) made a detailed study of child training in a Balinese village that, as a result of the outbreak of war, did not get as full a publication as it should have.

Among the actions they found was the mothers' regular practice of teasing their babies by fondling their genitals and, after they were aroused, withdrawing their attention and leaving the infant frustrated in its desire for affective response. They wrote, "the mother continually stimulates the child to show emotion—love or desire, jealousy or anger—only to turn away, to break the thread, as the child, in rising passion, makes a demand for some emotional response." They said that this leads to a sense of distrust of others and to a Balinese personality characterized by flat affect. They show the Balinese tendency to withdraw from contact with others in the many pictures they took with the then newly developed 36mm camera.

Inspired by this, I reviewed my Sebei[2] photographs to see if the maternal aloofness that I had sensed there could be documented (1976). A photograph I had taken of a handsome woman had long haunted me. She was walking along a path with a baby suckling at her breast, the palms of her hands not on the child and her eyes staring vacantly in the middle distance. It was a clear difference in affect from that shown by Mbuti of the Ituri forest I had visited, where both men and women constantly displayed affection toward the children. My photographs did show that Sebei women regularly hold their child by encircling it with their arms, the left hand grasping the right wrist so that neither hand is in contact with the baby. In the 28 photographs that depicted mothers holding infants (all taken without such purpose in mind), only one showed the mother making eye contact with her child or with her hand in contact with the child. This transmits a message of emotional disengagement and communicates a lack of affect in Sebei demeanor. This disengagement is reflected in the instrumental, unsentimental quality of their social institutions. No ritual that I attended was a happy affair, whether an initiation or a clan get-together, while the wedding rites seem calculated to intensify the

---

2. The Sebei are a tribal people of Uganda who had long been cattle-keeping pastoralists and who adopted the cultivation of plantains in the century or so prior to the British overrule. I studied (1976, 1986) their culture intensively, focusing on the social consequences of this shift. They will reappear in other contexts.

hostility between the bridal couple as well as between their respective clans, exacerbating the tensions of bride-price negotiations and Sebei sex relations.

Child development specialists had early found that Baganda babies were precocious in smiling and sitting up and thought this to be a natural (racial) talent. Kilbride et al. (1970) and Kilbride and Kilbride (1974) studied Baganda infant care practices and found that these accounted for this precocious behavior and tell us about the social institutions that explain it (1974). At the age of three months, Baganda children undergo a ritual in which they must be able to sit up. Success shows that the baby is a true member of the father's clan (i.e., a legitimate birth) and so one can see why the mother would be assiduous in training her babies for this event. This is not just ordinary behavioral imitation but a conscious social transmission of cultural attributes that relate to the dynamics of Baganda social life and show up in their graceful carriage as adults. Baganda also must maintain control of their body in front of their superiors, as demonstrated by the fact that a boy might be killed for breaking wind in the emperor's presence. Baganda adults also regularly smile to infants so as to induce them to smile and therefore infants are precocious in smiling, a trait that reflects the Baganda cultural desire to be ingratiating. Being ingratiating and having physical self-control were very important to success in traditional Baganda society, both at the domestic and the national level, so giving babies these traits had immediate and visible purpose.

We should look at the circularity between the experiences that lay down the child's earliest memories and the social institutions they support, for this circularity explains the adult's motivation to induce these subliminal sentiments in their infants. Buganda was a great empire, exerting its power over a large territory under the autocratic rule of the Kabaka (emperor) administered by a large organized bureaucracy and held together by a large army, the personnel for both of which was recruited from the peasantry. Thus any peasant's son could rise to great power and wealth, and many did. Getting the son to the court was a first step to success (as well as danger), and there was a constant flow of people from poverty to riches. A young man had to comport himself with great care and suck up to power with tact and self-control because the smallest breach might cost him his life. The same drama was played out in the peasant homes. Each proper household was under a domestic autocrat lording over his wives and children. Just as there was no designated nobility, there were no binding rules of inheritance and therefore any son of any wife who curried the father's favor could inherit his riches or get sent to court. Little wonder that the wives would urge their sons to learn the wiles to succeed at toadying. When I was last in Uganda, some 60 years after British overrule, the results of this cultural cycle were still apparent in the graceful carriage of Baganda men and women and I presume they remain so today. I watched the Baganda elite negotiate the terms of independence with the British colonial officers in 1962; they got all the terms they wanted from British officials—men who understood loyalty to queen and crown—who were presiding over this negotiation, only disastrously to lose control over Uganda soon after independence because they were not as adept at using the power as they were at knowing how to get it.

An Unanticipated Experiment

I want now to summarize contrasting analyses of the dynamics of infant care in the transmission of the subtle aspects of culture. This unanticipated natural experiment involves what I consider the best study of infancy ever made of a tribal society (of the Yurok Indians by psychoanalyst Erik Erikson, 1943) and my study of the neighboring and culturally identical Hupa. The two studies were both done with the sponsorship of Alfred Kroeber, whose work on the Yurok was extensive, a few years apart and entirely independent of one another. Kroeber had been a friend of Erikson and I was his student, but I didn't know Erikson then. No such comparison was in our minds, but each of us had been drawn to these peoples for their unusual and interesting culture, he by his commitment to Freudian theory and I because of the individuated pattern of social mobility.

The Yurok and Hupa were foragers inhabiting the rich valleys of the Humboldt and Trinity rivers that teemed with salmon; the valleys were rich in oak groves with their nutritious acorns and other food plants and game. The steep and forbidding mountains made for small communities in the narrow valleys and conflict was essentially internecine. The people lived in wood-plank houses in permanent villages of up to a hundred or so people. Unlike any other foragers I know of or, for that matter, any other tribal society, the Yurok and Hupa had a fluid social organization in which ownership of resources and a wide array of ceremonial treasures were the bases of influence, prestige, and power. They did not have fixed social units and no person's station in life was predetermined, though, of course, the well-born had advantages over sons of the less affluent. This open quality had drawn me to them and I later (1951) compared their culture to that described by Max Weber in *The Protestant Ethic and the Spirit of Capitalism* (1958). There was no marketplace as such, but wealth changed hands with the use of shell money; the competitiveness of market transaction took place in legal confrontations, for there was a veritable culture of litigation. The many laws offered an arena in which men regularly confronted one another and wealth was transferred to settle the disputes. Even the major food resources, special fishing locations, oak groves, and strategic hunting defiles were owned by specific households, and such property, as well as a rich variety of wealth goods, could be gained or lost through litigation. In good years food would be shared, but in bad ones it would be sold. Their money was dentalia, tooth-shaped sea-snail shells.

Instead of a Martin Luther, elaborate rituals and beliefs made very Protestant-like demands. These highly sacred rituals involved a wide range of paraphernalia, such as the skins of albino deer and yardlong flint or obsidian blades, which were privately owned and carefully hoarded measures of social standing. These community rites were designed to put back on an even keel the disc of the world that the evil weight of accumulated sins had tilted or, it was also said, to dispel the miasma of human sin that threatened to engulf the world. Ceremonies were led by self-selected men whose wealth in goods allowed them to claim the right to do so. They were not just showing off in some kind of conspicuous display but were displaying social alliances, for less wealthy men loaned their goods to one of the rich leaders to house that only knows unconditional love, belonging, and complete forgiveness.

TWO FATHERS

The Bible is very clear that there are two fathers: the father of lies and the Father of truth. Truth will always remind us of who we are and whose we are. Truth will always reinterpret our experience in a way that is congruent with how the Father thinks, feels, and sees. Truth helps us to feel what God feels and see ourselves and our experiences the way that God does. In my opinion, there is no better way out of lies than allowing God to speak truth into our lives.

The more that we grow accustomed to hearing God's voice and stop listening to unhealthy voices, the easier it becomes to live a healthy and empowered life in Him. The kingdom of darkness and the kingdom of light both work based on agreement: what we give our "yes" to will either empower lies or empower truth. This is why we must agree with what God says is true, because it has the power to untangle and circumvent years of suffering.

and cared for. However, what I am saying is that we often need to allow God to tell us a better story than the ones we have told ourselves. If not, we can stay stuck throughout our entire lives, believing lies about who we are and how we see ourselves. For example, say a woman was violated at a young age. It would be so easy to come out of that experience identifying as dirty or unlovable. These may feel true, but these feelings are 100% not in agreement with what God the Father is speaking over us. God never would say that about us, we said that about ourselves. No matter what has been done to us, or what we have done to others, God does not connect our experiences, pain, or even mistakes to our identity. The moment we mistakingly misplace our identity in what we have been through or in something we have done, we inevitably find ourselves ensnared in a web of lies. These lies are designed by the enemy to entangle us and distort our view of ourselves, and ultimately our view of life and God. The lies we believe always shrink our world and all God has for us, keeping us stuck in a prison of fear rather than being free in a house of love. The more we align our life and identity with God, the more comfortable we become living in God's house — a whom they felt allegiance. In this way these rituals were like "sociograms" of the power structure as of the moment. The subliminal drama of these lovely and sacred dances rendered the air electric with tensions, threats, and accusations that almost brought a halt to each of the ones that Harold Driver and I (who were present at successive occasions) attended. By reaffirming a structure for this unstructured society, the ritual does clarify and stabilize the society, as their figures of speech suggest, letting each person know just who stood with whom in the incessant quarrels that characterized their highly litigious world. Aside from a good inheritance or an advantageous marriage, the way to get rich was by taking every opportunity to press a suit, for which their law provides many such opportunities. There was no court; each delict was a tort mediated by a go-between according to strict rules of protocol for which the ultimate sanction was fighting between these fragile factions (Goldschmidt and Driver 1940).

These tribes truly had a Protestant ethic. Lust, sloth, gluttony, and any loss of self-control were not just frowned upon but were immoral and sinful, that is, breaches of conduct sanctioned by spiritual forces. Premarital celibacy was expected of both sexes and even a married man with many children was viewed as vulgar. The daily ritual sweat-bath followed by a dip in the icy river kept the men lean. They were a hard-working people, for industriousness was a prime virtue. Wealth was thus evidence of moral virtue, as in Protestant theology.

These customs are a prescription for creating an uptight people, a textbook example of the anal-erotic personality, which I assume is what drew Erikson to study them. According to Freudian theory, the anal-erotic personality has its origin in tensions around toilet training, especially bowel control, so Erikson "inquired into a possible emphasis on the time, place, or way of defecation, or into possible difficulties encountered in this part of child training." He goes on: "However, I only met with rather bland expressions, or even slight astonishment that anybody should see in these matters a problem per se" (1943:285). He notes that the parents show anxiety during the child-bearing process. A pregnant mother must eat little, work hard, and lean forward so that the fetus will not rest against her spine; toward the end of term she rubs her stomach to keep the fetus awake, and both parents are not to eat salmon or venison. The baby is not breast-fed for the first ten days and is weaned before it is a year old (very early for tribal people). The legs are massaged so that the child will begin creeping early. Consider what Erikson has found: high anxiety over food and control of appetite and of being energetic while the infant is *in utero* and after it is born but no anxiety whatsoever involving elimination of urine or feces.

These Yurok anxieties are transmitted in the subliminal discourse with children and enter into their intrinsic memories, creating a background mood of anxiety. But the Yurok know that the real indoctrination takes place when children reach what they call the "sense age." The Yurok determine that children have reached this sense age by repeatedly asking them if they can remember what they were told the day before; when they show with some regularity that they can, they are said to "have sense." This means that a child can now be held responsible for mistakes and, more relevant to our concerns, that the father is liable for any breach of Yurok law the child commits. Erikson depicts the self-control demanded of hungry six-year-olds in the grim daily rituals that take place at family meals with its focus on self-denial and visions of wealth (see Sidebar 7). Here the tie between self-control of the appetites and social rewards is made quite explicit. This is not as cynical as it sounds since, as we have seen, being wealthy is a religious virtue, as in Protestant theology. A Yurok thinking about money is as much prayer as avarice. Yet this is but one example of a severe moral code, for obedience and bodily self-control are strictly enforced. Yurok morality tales tell of the horrible consequences of disobedience, much like the old Struwelpeter stories of 19th-century Germany (which, incidentally, Erikson had referenced when he was describing German culture).

The parents want to have morally responsible children because an unruly child can prove costly in their litigious world. Driver and I, who had attended successive White Deerskin Dances, both learned the story of a quarrel between two children, one of whom had pushed the other into the ashes of a dead fire, which, in Hupa and Yurok belief, was a death-wish, for ashes are a symbol of death. Though the case had been formally settled, the tensions ran

A LESSON IN SELF-CONTROL

The first group of prohibitions and laws of conduct transmitted to the child as soon as this stage [of having sense] is reached concern the intake of food. He is told: "Eat slowly; don't grab food; never take food without asking for it; don't eat between meals; never eat a meal twice," and so on.

During meals a strict order of placement is maintained. Between the parents a space is always left for a potential guest. The girls sit near the mother, the boys near the father. The father teaches the boys and the mother the girls how to eat. They are told to take a little food with their spoon, to put it into their mouth slowly, to put the spoon back into the eating basket, and to chew slowly and thoroughly, meanwhile thinking always of becoming rich. Then the food is to be swallowed and the child may again reach, without haste, for the spoon. Nobody is supposed to talk during the meal, so that everybody can concentrate on thoughts of wealth. While there is still food in one's basket or in one's mouth, one does not ask for more. If a child eats too fast, the father or the mother silently takes his basket away from him and the child is supposed to rise silently and leave the house. Otherwise, the child is not allowed to leave ahead of any guest. Girls especially have to be patient, they remain sitting until first the guest, then the boys, then the father have left the room. . . .

In this compulsive way an attitude toward wealth is conditioned which later on allows the Yurok to think of wealth at any time in an almost hallucinatory way. When sitting or walking alone, he will always try to think of money or salmon, and he can make himself see money hanging from trees, even eating leaves or swimming in the river. In this way also an attitude is conditioned which encourages the Yurok to subordinate drive as such to the pursuit of wealth so that later on it will be not only his appetite for food which he learns to restrain for the sake of amassing wealth, but also his sexual desires.

Erikson 1943:286.

so high at the ceremony I attended that it almost came to a halt over unspoken hostilities. The complex legal case, in which each party had to pay indemnity to the other, was costly to the parents of both.

Erikson's description of Yurok childhood is remarkably sensitive to the tensions in Yurok life, as my brief summary of his description has shown, and he understandably tried to explain these tensions in Freudian terms. But his argument was a tall stretch. First, he extended the role in this Freudian paradigm from the anal sphincter to include the whole digestive tract, which he calls a tube, neglecting the fact that at its other end is the mouth, the focus of oral eroticism. Second, he sees evidence of the symbolic importance of the tube in various tribal practices as, for instance, the purse in which the Yurok keep their dentalia money. This purse is made of sections of hollow animal horn, which they close at each end, and then cut a slit in the side, through which they put their dentalia money. Because these slits are long, Erikson says they are, in effect, tubes. Clearly, this practice of inserting penis-shaped coins into a vagina-shaped slit can more readily symbolize the sex act than anything associated with the anus. Erikson has shown parental anxiety over eating, laziness, and sex, more or less in that order, and the denial of tensions regarding toilet training. It is clear that the Yurok *were* anxious parents who *did* transmit their anxieties to their children.

I have developed this in some detail because the crucial data that were collected by the eminent psychoanalyst himself cannot sustain the Freudian theories of child development but do support my thesis that parental anxieties transmitted during child-training are based on wishes to please the parents in their culture-based demands. That is, it is parents' nurturance that lies at the base of those cultural sentiments that are outside of their awareness. Thus, it disengages this paradigm from the sexual model of Freud and gives support to the model of nurturant love advocated here. The crucial evidence lies in the training that prepared children for the mental outlook required for the pursuit of the success in their particular culture. It shows that the child avidly seeks *ego* gratification rather than libidinal satisfaction.

Baganda child-training supports this model of infusing subliminal sentiments in the child during his first years that will direct him toward the appropriate behavior to fulfill the values of the culture and thus enable him to have a satisfying sense of self.

Bateson and Mead show that Bali parents are transmitting the peasants' need to conform to an existing rigidly hierarchical social order and in doing so are creating a passive peasantry with suppressed emotionality. My study of Sebei mothering is a sad commentary on the transmission of a social anomie that renders all social relations affectless and hence pragmatic and manipulative. And, while we are thinking about broad theoretical implications, we might turn back to Chagnon's simple-minded idea that Yanomamo ferocity is in their nature rather than being inculcated by some such cultural processes.

Affect and Adulthood

From infancy onward, boys and girls and men and women accept the demands made upon them because they want to be a part of the social world into which they happen to have been born. Affect hunger has induced them to do the things that get them the affective rewards they seek just as surely as the pangs of hunger will induce them to do what it takes to fill their stomachs. The ordinary hungers are directed at straightforward biological needs and are self-evident animal requirements. Affect hunger was the ingredient that was necessary for developing the mutuality that is essential to highly social animals; it does for sociality what sex does for reproduction. It differs from these other appetites in that the link is indirect and hidden. We are not cognizant of its operation, for its workings are subtle and indirect, and, as the satisfaction of this drive takes a wide variety of forms, its very existence goes unrecognized. What this thesis proclaims is that these motivations are, at base, the product of a biological phenomenon with deep evolutionary roots that has enabled our species to engage in acts that deny the fundamental law of evolutionary development.

We next examine the social and historical consequences of this phenomenon. We must remember, as we examine the superstructure that has been built on the edifice of affect hunger, that at base it is a physical desire and not itself a cultural element; that is, the transition from the physiology of affect to the symbolic expressions it receives in the cultural realities of life never fully slake the affective thirst. Before we proceed, however, I want to introduce a second syllogism that summarizes the basic lesson of this chapter:

- Every child is born into a socially constructed community with normative rules (culture).
- The child internalizes these rules of behavior and follows them in his daily activities.
- Therefore, every child acquires and acts on cultural motives.

6

Culture

The result of this revolution is that every Homo sapiens boy and girl that has ever lived gradually grows into a world constructed by those already there, getting to know who they are and how they fit in, how they are expected to behave and what might happen to them if they don't. This reality does not hit them at once but is absorbed over time and even may itself change. This is the world that we identify as culture and they will become part of that culture. In this situation, each person in the community is part of the social context of every other. This group of people, whose groupness has been defined by the very culture they are absorbing, is a "society"—a population trying to live in harmony to preserve their mutual interdependence in satisfying their material and emotional needs. Their life histories will be in the pursuit of those physical needs and desires that they have inherited as members of the species—food, shelter, protection, and sex—some of which they have already been seeking, as we have seen. They will also be in pursuit of those social needs and desires for affective response from those around them. These responses, which at the outset were overwhelmingly physical and direct and which were induced in part by their own charms, become increasingly detached from physicality and increasingly offered in more symbolic form, as the social world expands and comes to dominate their interests. In this way they are gradually slotted into the statuses and roles to which they have been assigned and move on to other ones as the passage of time makes possible and as their changing situation and their own efforts make available. We should keep this fluidity in mind as we discuss culture, for the inevitable fixity of a description tends to make us lose sight of it.

Definition of Culture

The word "culture" has a long and convoluted history and has a way of changing from place to place and even, if one is not careful, from sentence to sentence. It has in the past meant the contents of a petri dish and the knowledge of the sophisticated class. Archaeologists use it to delineate separate layers in their research sites. The business community now talks of "corporate cultures." As I shall use the word, it is unique to humans, though, as we have seen and as we should expect, many of its individual attributes are found among other social animals. The anthropologists' concept of culture was forged in the study of simpler, homogeneous societies, and it is easier to see how it works by thinking of its operation with the tribe in mind.[1]

Culture is therefore the shared perception of the universe and its contents, seen as a systemic whole, including the perceptions of self and the delineation of behavioral propriety. This perception is not limited to the senses but includes the feelings and the emotional tonus, insofar as these are also shared—shared, that is, by members of a population that accepts a common definition of itself as a unity. These perceptions of the universe are internalized during the long period of maturation, as we discussed in the last chapter. They are not identical in the minds of each member of the community, though the people act as if they were. People try to preserve this image of conformity, much of which is embedded in their shared language and supported by community ritual and other social institutions.

We may call this cultural universe the "symbolic world" or we may think of it as the original "cyberspace"—that is, as a creation

---

1. While the special genius of anthropology derives from its early and intense involvement with nonliterate people, it was never limited to them as a source of understanding, as its early history shows.

of the human mind. What we know of the physical world comes to us through the very limited and narrow channels of our five senses. (Modern science has abetted this not with adding new senses to our repertoire but by finding a means to record other wavelengths, such as X rays and subsonic and supersonic sound, into modalities that we can perceive.) To these have been added the conceptual entities that we create, such as social units, mystical entities, and metaphysical notions, all of which are given symbolic reality, labeled with what we call words, and put together into meaningful utterances that we call "sentences," ultimately to be built into the myths, essays, and narratives like this one that I have written and you are reading. These narratives give us the structure of the world as we know it—the physical, the metaphysical, and the imaginary, the people and even ourselves—all mixed together in one great imagined universe. We are all living our symbolic lives in a symbolic world. That is the ultimate view of what culture is, as will become more explicit in the discussion that follows.

Whatever we call them, cultures are the worlds within which all normal people operate. This is not to say people are cultural automatons any more than they are biologically programmed beasts. Rather, it is to say that people know, and are expected to know, when behavior does not conform to local expectations. If the breach is sufficiently gross, they will expect a penalty, whether by loss of face, property, limb, or life. There will, nevertheless, be breaches because customary expectation may run counter to personal desires or animal appetites. Culture does not eliminate the animal urges that came into being in the interest of survival, but where the two conflict, the cultural expectations will get the support of the community and thus have a moral priority. Where the two are at odds, courses of action must be chosen.

The culture of a people includes much that is obvious in their lives. It includes the cumulated knowledge of how to make a living from the landscape; how to protect themselves from the hazards it creates, including those created by their human neighbors; and what they believe about the world around them and about themselves and the rules of conduct that the members are expected to follow. These are the specifics that get varied from place to place and from time to time. This needs to be said but not dwelt upon because it raises no major issues for us. We are here more interested in culture as a phenomenon.

Language as Communication of Cultural Understanding

Language encodes the nature of the universe as the speakers know it. As every human being acquires most cultural attributes through language, we must revisit the matter of what language is and what it does. Earlier I separated language from other forms of animal communication by showing that its grammar frees discourse from the prison of the immediate present and enables people to formulate (and thereby share) a view of that part of the universe of which they are aware. These views include both that physical reality which we perceive with our senses (sometimes called the real world) and the world as it is perceived through the lenses of culture. These two worlds are always entangled and transmitted from parent to child as if they were a unified whole, so they are conflated in people's minds. People everywhere dwell in such language-defined worlds.

There is a dynamic interrelation between what we say and what we think. When anthropologists began to study the languages of the exotic peoples they found a wider range of grammatical forms than those Western philologists knew, and some contained different metaphysical preconceptions. They felt that these linguistic forms shaped perceptions for the speakers as they were learning them. The eminent linguist Edward Sapir was by no means the first to realize this when he wrote: "The worlds in which different societies live are distinct worlds, not merely the same world with different labels attached" (1929:209).

This concentration on linguistic differences was made at the cost of inadequate attention to the common elements in language. Noam Chomsky, a psychologist whose studies made him aware that infants easily and quickly learn the complexities of speech in the first two or three years of life merely by hearing it spoken, realized that the human brain must have an inherent capacity for learning grammar. Chomsky called it a "universal grammar" and so was denying cultural differences, making the same mistake in reverse that the anthropological linguists had made in failing to see linguistic constants. In *The Language Instinct,* psychologist Stephen Pinker (1994) dismisses Sapir's work by confusing the natural capacity for learning grammar with the specific grammar that is learned. Pinker and Sapir are talking past one another. Sapir was talking about *what* we think, about the *mind,* for that is an anthropological question, while Pinker is talking about *how* we think, about the *brain,* but he was too busy refuting what he knows nothing about to realize it.

Let us look at how speech affects perceptions. Very subtly, language structures our thoughts and so unconsciously shapes our views of such basic matters as time, space, and agency. To speak a language is to be caught up in its preconceptions. Most of what people "know" is what they have been told rather than experienced, and what they are told is contaminated by the conceptions that are embedded in the language in which they learned it. Navaho, for instance, constructs its sentences around the verb, in contrast to Indo-European languages, where the subject is dominant. This, linguist Harry Hoijer argued, is related to the Navaho's sense of subordination to the forces of nature. Navaho would say what we would normally say of Joe while watching a football game something like, "watching football is the condition of Joe." When sentences are regularly constructed this way, it constantly reinforces the deep philosophic presumption of the actor not causing the action, but being affected by it—as persons being subordinate to nature. More broadly, this also recognizes that actions are always contextual, which our language doesn't do. This attitude lies deep in the Navaho outlook, whereas Indo-European languages normally put the actor in charge. The Indo-European way puts the subject as implicitly determining what is taking place in the sentence, giving emphasis to the sense of agency and independent action.

I pointed out earlier that words deal with *classes* of things or actions, whether "real" or not. But to dismiss classes as being *mere* constructs is to fail to recognize the physical reality that is there, if often somewhat misrepresented. What we must do is to "deconstruct" them, if need be, as I did earlier for the word "love." We must realize when and in what way a taxon reflects physical reality. Consider two taxonomies: race and gender. Race refers to a variety of people distinguished by attributes assumed to be inherent, basically such superficial things as pigmentation and hair texture. These differences formed the basis of racial classifications and were assumed to be correlated with traits of real significance, such as character or intelligence, also thought to be inherited. The appeal of this perception lie in its "justification" for the harsh treatment of slaves, natives, and immigrants. None of the presumed correlations such as those in the recent *The Bell Curve* (Herrnstein and Murray 1994) stand up to scientific scrutiny. Anthropology got caught in these folk notions early in its development and tried to create racial taxonomies that would have some biological consistency, but they could not agree on any system that made any sense and the effort slowly disappeared in the 1930s. But the notion of race is so ingrained in our language that even those who are fighting racial stereotypes must use the terminology. Race is a construct.

Gender, on the other hand, is a distinction of importance in nature, based on essential physical features and physiological functions and, to state the obvious, is necessary to the survival of the species. Treating gender as "merely" a social construct like race denies its biological reality. Of course, the genders are encrusted with socially constructed attributes and with culturally defined meanings.[2] I also like to think of university catalogues as a kind of taxonomy of the world of knowledge. Examining a sample of them over the past century would show how our perception of the universe has altered.

To see how subtly language expresses and therefore influences deep-seated attitudes, I want to call attention to a small but significant linguistic shift that has occurred during my lifetime, at least for a sector of our own culture. In the sixties a small, amusing, but

---

2. The fact that some people are born with the physical features of one gender and the self perception of the other so that they seek operations that will resolve their conflict does not invalidate the categories. Our language provides a word for such situations, "anomaly," which is regularly used for items that fit poorly into any category.

important change of phrasing occurred along with the change in sexual mores from a strict taboo against sexual intercourse between unmarried couples to its wide acceptance and the related matter of whether women get pleasure in sex or are reluctant partners. The old pattern treated dating as a kind of contest in which the boy sought sex and the girl defended herself from his pursuit of it. This sense of confrontation was expressed in a standard query from the roommate upon returning from a date, "Did you *make* her?" With the change in mores, this sexist question became, "Did you *make out*?" Same pronoun, same verb; different subject, different predicate. The pronoun shifts from singular to plural, conveying mutuality, the predicate from transitive to intransitive as sex is now seen as a shared experience and no longer seen as a male conquest. The change in wording came in response to the change in mores, but once in place, the new expression replaced the subliminal message that was expressed by my generation of college students. To be sure, this was only one way in which sexual attitudes are subtly embedded in the language, and I am not sure all expressions of conquest have been eliminated. But I suspect that, despite classes in sex education, most of what boys and girls still learn about sexual attitudes they get from their peers, as was clearly the case in my youth. This example shows that language influences outlook in an entirely subliminal way and yet is amenable to change in response to new imperatives. It preserves culture's special advantage: flexibility.

Ritual as Communication of Cultural Sentiment

In an earlier chapter, I noted that humans have two modalities of communication, and we must now look at how communication can help unify affect. Our first affective experiences are within the bosom of the family, most particularly in mother–infant dialogues. We have already seen these in action and how they transmitted sentiments appropriate to participation in the ambient cultures of the Hupa, Yurok, and Baganda. Some of this early use of voice and gesture carries into verbal language in common use and remains throughout verbal discourse, so much so that language can be laden with feeling—both positive and negative.

But only a skillful orator can make his listeners *feel* the way he feels, however clearly they *understand* what he feels. To achieve a unity of sentiment it takes group action in the form of ritual. We think of rituals as essentially sacred, but they may be secular. Erikson's description of the Yurok family meal is a secular ritual, designed to communicate the imperative need for self-restraint to their children—though, of course, there is an underlying spiritual message. I have no difficulty appreciating this, for dinner was also a learning experience in behavior and morals in my natal household, though the lesson there was more "eat your food up" than "not so fast." (I still find it hard to leave food on my plate, the echo of "think of the starving Armenians" still in my ears.) The Baganda sitting-up ceremony is overtly sacred, despite its profane purpose.

The best way I can think of to make you understand how rituals make the participants feel is to try to make *you* feel what a ritual communicates by giving you samples of a description. I will borrow from a dramatic presentation from Ruth Benedict's description of the rituals of two peoples in her classic *Patterns of Culture* (1934),[3] because she had the poetic talent to catch the drama involved. She is depicting the Kwakiutl "Dionysian" cannibal society initiation with its intense and fearful enactment of the cannibals' presumed activities, for the Kwakiutl share our horror of cannibalism. You will readily see the contrast with the Zuni "Apollonian" initiation into a Kiva society, with its quiet mood and subliminal sense of community and equality. It is clear that the Kwakiutl are dramatizing the fearfulness of the world and creating a mood for personal aggression in handling interpersonal relationships in a society that values the competitive spirit while the Zuni want their children to suppress their competitive ego drives in favor of the sense the mutual interdependence, so necessary to their desert existence (see Sidebars 8 and 9).

---

3. *Patterns of Culture* was the bellwether for the public understanding of the cultural paradigm, contrasting the cultural psychology of the Kwakiutl, Zuni, and Dobuans with rich descriptions of their respective cultures. As in all my quoted material, I have not indicated elisions but always put any supplied words in brackets.

PUEBLO APOLLONIAN INITIATION CEREMONY

Membership in one or the other of [the] kivas follows from the choice of a boy's ceremonial father at birth, but there is no initiation till the child is between five and nine years old. This initiation . . . does not teach him esoteric mysteries; it establishes a bond with supernatural forces. It makes him strong, and, as they say, valuable. The "scare kachinas," the punitive masked gods, come for the initiation, and they whip the children with their yucca whips. It is a rite of exorcism, "to take off the bad happenings," and to make future events propitious. In Zuni whipping is never used as a corrective of children.

When the boy is about fourteen and old enough to be responsible, he is whipped again by even stronger masked gods. It is at this initiation that the kachina mask is put upon his head, and it is revealed to him that the dancers are in reality his neighbors and his relatives. After the final whipping, the four tallest boys are made to stand face to face with the scare kachinas who have whipped them. The priests lift the masks from their heads and place them upon the heads of the boys who face them, now with the masks put upon their heads. They are commanded to whip the kachinas. It is their first object lesson in the truth that they, as mortals, must exercise all the functions which the uninitiated ascribe to supernaturals themselves.

Benedict 1934:69–70.

Benedict had no interest in explaining why these cultures are so different, but I do, for the two emotional demands of each relate to their respective ecological circumstances. Rituals use the raw materials of our sensory input to make us feel the way our community wants us to feel. Some of these are immediate, as a war dance to psych men up for battle, while others are more generic, to infuse a mood or attitude in the youth who are entering adult culture, as in these cases. The transition from childhood to adulthood often involves major life changes and many peoples help this transition with special initiation rites. Harmony was essential to life among the Pueblo Indians of the American Southwest, living crowded together in apartmentlike dwellings and scratching out a hard living by cultivating small plots of corn, beans, and squash. The fate of one really was the fate of all. Benedict called them

KWAKIUTL DIONYSIAN INITIATION CEREMONY

[When] the period of his seclusion was drawing to an end, the tribe were preparing for the Winter Dance which was primarily [the neophytes's] initiation as a member of the Cannibal Society. The people of the tribe called among them the spirits of the Winter Dance, and those who had a right to do so gave demonstrations of their supernatural frenzy. Their power must be great enough to call back the Cannibal from his sojourn with the supernaturals. They called him by strong dances and by the exercise of inherited powers, but at first all their efforts were in vain.

At last all the Cannibal Society by their combined frenzy roused the new initiate, who all of a sudden was heard upon the roof of the house. He was beside himself. He shoved aside the boards of the roof and jumped down among all the people. In vain they tried to surround him. He ran around the fire and out again by a secret door, leaving behind him only the sacred hemlock branches he had worn. All the [society members] followed him toward the woods, and presently he was seen again. Three times he disappeared, and on the fourth an old man went out ahead, "the bait," as he was called. The Cannibal rushed upon him, seized his arm, and bit it. The people caught him in the act and brought him to the house where the ceremonial was to be held. He was out of his senses and bit those whom he laid hold of. When they came to the ceremonial house he could not be made to enter. At last the woman whose duty it was to carry the prepared body across her arms appeared naked with the corpse. She danced backward, facing the Cannibal, enticing him to enter the house. He still could not be prevailed upon, but at length he again climbed the roof and jumped down through the displaced boards. He danced wildly, not able to control himself, but quivering in all his muscles in the peculiar tremor which the Kwakiutl associate with frenzy.

By different rites of exorcism they tried to "reach" the Cannibal in his ecstasy. The final exorcism was performed with the menstrual blood, [which was seen as] polluting to a degree hardly excelled in the world. Women were secluded during this period, and their presence rendered any shamanistic practice impotent. They could not step across any brook nor go near the sea lest the salmon take offence. Deaths which occurred in spite of shamanistic cures were regularly laid to the unsuspected presence in the house of cedar bark upon which there was a trace of menstrual blood. For the final exorcism of the Cannibal, therefore, the priest took cedar bark upon which there was menstrual blood of four women of the highest rank, and smoked the face of the Cannibal. As the exorcism took effect the dancing of the Cannibal became more sober, until upon the fourth dance he was tamed and quiet, his frenzy gone from him.

Benedict 1943:179–181.

Apollonian. They initiated several children together, symbolizing in several ways the virtue of mutuality and suppression of individuality. The contrast to the Northwest Coast Kwakiutl is clear; the one young man being initiated is out of control and engaging in horrifying antisocial behavior, his individual demands being brought under control with great difficulty by using the fearful symbols of magical power: cannibalism and menstrual blood. This neophyte is facing far greater dangers than merely the wild animals and human enemies that he will later encounter.

Anybody who has gone through the Marine Corps boot camp will know the powerful force of ritual indoctrination. I could see it among the Sebei, where the hardships of joint circumcision rites created strong bonds even 50 years after their social purpose had been lost. I have seen evidence of such survival of attitudes that had been acquired by children long after the elders had given up their cultural practices, showing how resistant to change attitudes can be that had been laid down with the emotional powers of ritual performance. The California Indians still call on the Hupa and Yurok to lead fights in their battles in Sacramento, in recognition of their superior skill in social manipulation. One example of the strength of ritual imprinting was expressed in the memory of a Tlingit woman, whose knowledge of land ownership was learned while a maiden at a potlatch some 60 years earlier, whereas those rights that had been set down in the records of the Alaska territorial office had been forgotten.

Careers

I have stressed throughout that human beings are neither biological automatons nor cultural robots. The fundamental advantage to the peculiar human style of life lies in the adaptations individuals can make to situational conditions; if culture had merely substituted one form of control for another our species would not have succeeded in conquering the whole world.

Underlying this adaptability is the autonomy of the individual. People differ by nature; people differ in the experiences that shape them; each person takes his own path through the maze he traverses toward his own inevitable death. Each culture presents opportunities and offers its own rewards. Though tribal societies offer few alternatives, they do exist—even if only to refuse to go along with the expected, as we shall see in a later context. Each individual not only enters into a group with established rules of behavior and ideas of propriety but also develops his own agenda as to what he wants to do and wants to avoid, an agenda that grows and changes but is always in the service of self-interest. This agenda is built upon the biological urges for food, sex, and physical comfort and affective responses and the cultural urges to behave in ways that will serve the symbolic gratification through acceptance, social standing, and the public expressions of approval in a symbolic way.

The central drama in human life revolves around this pursuit of a sense of self that is found in the appropriate performance of the social roles into which he has been cast by the structural features of the society in which he lives. Humans spend most of their lives in a kind of drama that serves to meet the need for this self-definition. Usually and ideally, these actions contribute not only to the individual's physical needs and wants but also to the welfare of the community, whether by helping to provision it or in its defense or meeting other social requisites. The urge to do this and the means by which it is achieved are largely laid down in that infantile discourse of early life, now translated from maternal nurturance to the approval of the fellow citizens—for it is their judgments that are the basis for each person's self-evaluation. Such expressions of approval are not the physical contacts of infancy but are various kinds of markers, either verbal, like titles and sobriquets, or physical, like goods and "wealth"—status markers.

In this drama of daily life, the sets and props vary, the action varies and can be more or less intense, but the plot is always fundamentally the same: Will the protagonist get the affect gratification he or she is seeking? The characters are those selves we have already met; they are the puppets manipulated by the very humans they represent. The culture writes the script and the society provides the supporting cast, each one, in its turn, playing out its own drama.[4] How this affect is expressed, what the heroes and heroines must do to get these expressions of affect, and the hazards and challenges they face are what vary from culture to culture, like variations on the Cinderella story in the movies. The aim is not just to get the boy/girl; for, in order really to "live happily ever after," one must get those tokens that represent public approval (and thus assurance) of one's competence. I once thought that the tokens marking success had to relate directly or indirectly to productive behavior, as cows do among the Sebei, but one often must strain to find a connection. Why, for instance, do the Hupa measure social standing by the amount of ceremonial goods they have horded while farther north on the Pacific coast it is measured by giving things away with excessive abandon? Why in some societies is military prowess and fearlessness praised and elsewhere accolades are given for piety and self-effacement? Why do some honor sexual prowess and others celibacy? While the competitive drama is more intense in some societies than others, I have yet to read of a people who give no evidence of such drama; it has been seen in slave quarters and concentration camps, where the rules of the game are contextualized by the demands of the captors but nevertheless play a significant role in the inhabitants' quotidian lives.

Men and women are both involved in this drama. The dramas of the men loom larger in the ethnographic literature, in no small measure because men have done most of the reporting. Annette Weiner's demonstration that the Trobriand women had commerce in status symbols that mirrored the famous Kula ring but was unreported in the voluminous work of Malinowski suggests as much. I think, however, that women's role in reproduction may give them so much affect gratification that the public drama has

---

4. I made some verbatim records of Sebei social events that show scenes of these daily dramas in which one can see the diverse aims of the several players (Goldschmidt 1966, 1972).

less appeal. The recent entry of women into the drive for self-definition through "gainful employment" (what a sneaky put-down to the often more demanding task of raising a family!) makes it clear that women do have the competence and temperament to succeed in such public spheres of activity, which our cultural traditions long denied them. Some women have recognized that this activity comes at a cost to the old source of affect gratification to the extent that they take on both burdens. The change in women's participation has come after the dangers, hardships, and accolades for having successful babies declined and as the conditions of the workplace got more enticing. Many cultures give high marks to successful mothering, as did our own before it was denigrated by the women's rights movement.[5]

Reinforcement

Cultural unity does not just happen. The encounters and conflicts in tribal life attest to the fact that people vary. When behavior threatens the sanctity of the established order, the elite with the power to do so—that is, of course, the very people who are benefiting by the traditions—will take measures to enforce the rules. Thus culture is not only inculcated, but reinforced when deemed necessary. Ritual, preaching, and morality tales are the standard procedure, but more Draconian measures are also used. Rousseau's sentimentalized idea of man in nature living in harmony and equality is as false as Hobbes's "war of each against all" or the "short and brutish savage life." Evidence that tribal life is not harmonious is often dismissed as being the product of Western influence (which does undermine native practices), and that is why I have put a selection from the work of Sir Baldwin Spencer and F. J. Gillen (1904) on the Arunta (now Aranda) in Sidebar 10. It is in such detail that it

---

5. This is not to be read as criticism of the women's rights movement, which came out of the cultural devaluation of motherhood in general and the increased social attractiveness of the workplace. It is a shame that the cultural relativism anthropologists regularly apply elsewhere could not have been used for both the professional and the domestic roles of modern women.

ABORIGINAL JUSTICE

When all was prepared the Atninga [avenging party] came upon a group of Iliaura men, consisting of about a dozen families. The Iliaura sent some of their women over to the strangers' camp, but the use of the women was declined. The Iliaura community [sent] two old men [to confer.] After a long talk extending over two days, the [Atninga leaders] gave the Iliaura men very clearly to understand that they were determined to exact vengeance, the two old men said, in effect, "Go no further. Our people do not wish to quarrel with your people; there are three bad men in our camp whom we Iliaura do not like, they must be killed. Two are *Iturka* (men married [in] forbidden degrees of relationship); the other is very quarrelsome and strong in magic and has boasted of killing your people by means of magic. Kill these men, but do not injure any others in our camp, and we will help you."

These terms were accepted by the Arunta, and it was agreed that an attempt should be made to kill the three men on the next day. At daylight the old men of the Iliaura went some little distance away from their camp, and there made a special fire, at which it is intended to surprise and kill the men who have been condemned. Shortly after daylight a number of [unarmed] Arunta, led by an old man, went over to the [fire] and took special care to engage the condemned men in conversation. The remainder of the Atninga party in full war-paint, with whittled sticks in their hair, their bodies painted with red ochre, carrying spears, boomerangs, and shields, and each one wearing the magic girdle made of a dead man's hair, crept up unseen and, suddenly springing up, speared two of the condemned men from behind. The third man—one of the two ["incestuous" men] had grown suspicious during the night, and had accordingly decamped, taking his women with him.

A large number of spears were thrown into the bodies of the men who were killed. [Then] the Atninga party danced round the bodies, and taking the whittled sticks from their heads, broke them up and threw the pieces on to the bodies. The Iliaura men looked on quietly while the killing took place, and when all was over, the spears were taken out of the bodies by the men who had acted as decoys and handed back to their owners, [lest] some great evil befall them, as the body of a victim and anything in contact with it killed in this way is strictly tabu to the killer.

> The [avenging party] took the [wife] of one of the dead men, and she became and is now the property of the old man who seized her. One girl child was annexed by one of the younger men, who carried her on his back for the greater part of the return journey.
>
> Spencer and Gillen 1927:444–445.

must have been witnessed before central Australia had been seriously impacted by Europeans (late 19th century). In fact, the actions are so engulfed in ritual that they must have been an ancient practice.

Consider this event; consider first the need for such a system of control, men and women defying one of the most sacred taboos of their society. It shows that many men and women were not following the standard Aranda script. Then consider the devious way these revered elders acted. There is an uncanny feeling of modernity in the apparently cynical use of power, but one may credit the elders as seeing themselves as nobly preserving sacred custom against the youthful disregard of the sacred—a justification always set forth to make harsh measures seem right. Consider also that, in all the anthropological discussion of Australian kinship systems, I have never seen reference to this singular event, though two of the targets of this execution were men who had flouted the very rules of marriage in the elaborate kinship system that had been endlessly discussed. Remember, two families had been living in the intimate environment of a band of about a dozen married couples; four such "sinners" out of no more than two dozen people constitute a large fraction of the population. Nor was this a unique event. The authors tell us that this mode of rendering justice was a common practice often applied to this very delict: "When a case of this kind arises, the old men of the group . . . hold a meeting to discuss the matter, and if all of them are in favour of the death of a man or woman, a neighbouring group is asked to come and carry out the sentence" (Spencer and Gillen 1927:446). That it was a hallowed mode of punishment is shown by the detailed ritual cleansing that had to be undergone to avoid contamination from their dubious role—and suggests some guilt feeling as well. Yet the authors who described this scene can still say that "the Australian native is bound hand and foot by custom" (Spencer and Gillen 1937:11). Anthropologists have their own myths.

Cultural Adaptability

Cultural attitudes are tenacious but not immutable. Indeed, if they were not changeable there would be no use to give up the reliability of hard circuitry for the uncertainties of cultural response. Cultures must meet the conflicting demands of behavioral stability and situational adaptability. Balancing between the traditional and the adaptive is a recurrent source of tension in human history. Such tensions are best seen when examining change, and so we will look at evidence drawn from a study in East Africa by a team I organized in 1961.

It is worth pausing for a brief reflection. I entered anthropology during the Depression; very little firsthand research among tribal people not living on reservations had been done since early in the century, so we were still using perceptions from the past. This was not helped by the anthropological tradition of describing cultures as if the traditional events were still going on, which came to be called "the ethnographic present." This had the subliminal effect of denying the pastness of traditional behavior. Another consequence was to conceptualize the "tribe" as a clearly bounded entity, disregarding variation. In retrospect, both the Hupa and the Tlingit had clearly recognized sectors that had slightly varied customs that I never mentioned. For some purposes, including my uses here, this doesn't really matter, but it is relevant in discussing social processes.

When I first went to the Sebei in 1954, I was still caught in this false perception, though admittedly by then I should not have been. When I began going over my field notes, I became aware that the Sebei had a lot of behavioral diversity and realized that much of it was because of the shift in economy from cattle pastoralism to hoe farming that took place before the British colonized Uganda, in which some sectors clung more firmly to the old traditions while others had converted almost entirely to farming. Furthermore, I realized that these internal variations were adaptations to environmental conditions, for the conservative divisions occupied the arid plain most suitable to grazing cattle, while the farmers lived on the side of well-watered Mount Elgon where plantains could be cultivated. Sebei culture was caught in mid-stride, like a camera catching a runner in mid-air, when colonialism put an end to the process of native adaptation. That is, they were one "tribe" in that old perception, and they shared language and customs, but they were living two fundamentally different lifestyles.

Meanwhile, I had written *Man's Way* (1959), in which I developed my theory of cultural evolution, which sees ecological adaptation as the driving force and technological advancement as altering the ecological equation, giving evolution its "upward" thrust. I realized that in Sebei I had an example of the consequences of technological change on social life. I did not have to make the assumption that one was an evolutionary "advancement" over the other, but only wanted to observe what processes were involved when such changes occurred. Here was a "natural experiment" to test these ideas, and I organized The Culture and Ecology Project with a six-man team to study four "tribes" (including Sebei) of East Africa who had made this ecological shift. Pastoralism and hoe farming are adapted to different environments and make very different task demands that call for different forms of collaboration, and these create new kinds of social problems. They even favor different types of personality. I will draw on this experience to show some facets of this cultural adaptation.

Sebei pastoralists live off their herds and flocks, and the aim of each man is to build up his herd and to use his animals to buy wives by which to have many children. Other than stock, possessions mean nothing and land is a public good that is available to whoever has cattle. As the animals must be moved to where there is grass and water (rainfall is always uncertain in areas devoted to stock-keeping), life is nomadic within a broadly defined tribal territory. How much movement will vary from one tribe to another, but most animal herders have little investment in a locality or with a fixed set of people; they defend their animals in intertribal conflict rather than protect a home territory. The age-sets that are formed among the men who had been circumcised together lead to strong male bonding, and this creates warrior groups of young men to raid and counterraid their neighbors' stock. The men retain this bond as they become the governing elders when they are old. In contrast, each farmer's prosperity depends upon his land holdings, and a man wants to gain access to land and protect it from others. This offers a fertile ground for strife among people who can no longer take their capital elsewhere to avoid conflict, strife for which the old controls no longer functioned and new ones had not yet been perfected when the British colonial office took things in hand. The permanent residence of concentrated farmers pressures them to get along with their neighbors, and yet conflict over land was endemic.[6]

Many changes went along with this basic shift, but I find the transformation of *misisi* into *mukutanek* (see Sidebar 11) the most intriguing precisely because it was a ritual of such little apparent significance. My informant started by telling me who was invited to misisi, implying that it was a ritual of explicitly social purpose. Indeed, it was; it was a low-key peace-making ritual for people who were unavoidably involved with one another but had a lot of opportunity for conflict. The guest list for the original misisi consisted mostly of in-laws—persons whose company one could not disavow and yet with whom one had almost unavoidable tension over unmet obligations. Bride-price bargaining and the marriage ceremonies themselves were so filled with hostility-provoking acts that one wonders that these families ever sat around the beer pot together. The shift to mukutanek went with the growth of agriculture and the guest list changed to a new source of tension: from in-laws to neighbors. In a world where boundaries are marked off only by special plants that could secretly be moved and often were, conflict was endemic, as my data verified. My experience of the mukutanek when I got to participate in it was to find everyone being most decorous, unlike the usual raucous beer-parties I had attended. I find great meaning in this undramatic little rite (about as exciting as a Thanksgiving dinner), for it shows how people can change traditions as needs change.

---

6. For details on this research, see Goldschmidt (1976, 1986) and Edgerton (1971).

RITUAL ADAPTATION

Conflict between neighbors was so endemic among the agricultural Sebei that they transformed an old family ritual of amity, *misisi*, into a neighborhood gathering, *mukutanek*. It is an example of how institutions are subtly reshaped to meet new exigencies.

Misisi used to take place in October after the millet was harvested. The grain is plucked in the head, and the ears are set out on mats to dry in the sun and then put, still in the head, in granaries. Some grain falls off, and these gleanings, called *misisi*, are collected and used for making beer for the harvest rite that took its name from these gleanings. *Misisi* was a feast with food as well as beer, and a bullock if it could be afforded. Libations of beer were poured for the ancestral spirits by the host's father, who says, "By brewing this beer, we say that there had been darkness and now light is coming with the new crops." The good spirits are offered beer inside the house and are mentioned by name; they include the host's fathers, brother, mother, mother's brothers, grandparents, fathers-in-law, brothers-in-law, and all the deceased members of the host's clan whose names are known and who have living descendants. A failure to mention an ancestor might annoy the spirit. Libations are poured for the evil spirits away from the house or *kraal*, using the left instead of the right hand; evil spirits may also be mentioned by name and will include those relatives who have died without progeny and are therefore jealous, or those who cursed a kinsman when he was alive. They are thus placated but kept at a distance.

As with Thanksgiving feasts among us, the relationships among the living are also served. The guest list proper to *misisi* specifically included an age-set mate, a *tilyet* [cattle partner], a sister's daughter's husband and his brothers, and, for each wife, her father, brothers, mother's brother, their wives, and her daughter's husband. These are all persons with whom there is mutual obligation and respect, but also a certain degree of tension. Little wonder then that the songs they sing around the beer pot are all circumspect, not vulgar like those sung during initiations, and the demeanor is polite and restrained.

This ritual was transformed into *mukutanek*, the new word derived from sharing. Though one family acts as host and prepares the beer, each has supplied some of the maize and millet out of which it is made. More importantly, the guest list is changed; kinsmen have largely been replaced by neighbors. These represent the

95

new sources of tension in a farming community, tensions that derive from the kinds of disputes [over boundaries] and from the more petty everyday conflicts that are apt to characterize social interaction in this crowded land.

Goldschmidt 1986:52–54.

There were, of course, many more significant changes. The pastoralists gave up the large, fenced camps to live in houses scattered over the land, as our American farmers do, shifting military operations from the raiding and counterraiding by young herder-warriors to the defense of the now stable homeland by all able-bodied men. This, in turn, undermined the age-set system that was already losing its importance when I was there and had left an unfilled power vacuum. There was some vague evidence of there having been a period shortly before the British took over in which clansmen settled into neighborhoods together, with the implication that they would farm the land in some clan-controlled mutual way, but it is not clear how far this developed. It ran counter to one of the dominant aspects of the earlier cattle-keeping Sebei ethos: the strong sense of independence and self- help that ran against the grain of accepting the administrative control of clan elders.

The psychological profiles of the two sectors varied in ways we had anticipated. The circumstances of pastoral life make for a relatively open emotionality, people having to take immediate action when attacked and free to speak out against neighbors, but also free to move away if unhappy with their fellow campers. Farmers do not have such freedom to suppress their anger. Robert Edgerton (1971), who gave a battery of tests to evoke expressions of values, sentiments, and psychological attributes from samples of both men and women from both pastoral-oriented and farmer-oriented villages in each of the four tribes we studied, corroborated this hypothesis (see Sidebar 12). We know that these more subliminal aspects of culture can be very tenacious despite changes; it is interesting to see that they can also be adaptable to altered circumstances; that lifestyle can help shape personality attributes.

PSYCHOLOGICAL ADAPTATION

At the most general level of comparison, I believe that farmers and pastoralists are differentiated on two dimensions: (1) open versus closed emotionality, and (2) direct versus indirect action. These dimensions—themes, perhaps—appear to me to find expression primarily as psychological sets, although they also serve as general orienting principles of the kind sometimes referred to as world view, or value orientation. . . .

To illustrate what I have in mind in these two dimensions of comparison, [consider] the emotionality of farmers. The emotions of farmers may well be strongly felt—indeed, there is every evidence that they are—but they are not openly expressed. Perhaps I should say that they are not readily revealed, for it seems that farmers are actively engaged in conscious concealment of their true feelings. It is my impression that farmers tend to withhold emotional expression because of their calculation that it is in their best interest to do so. For the most part, farmers seem to succeed in closing off their emotions to others, for it is only now and then that suppressed feelings break through in impulsive, uncontrolled fashion. And when this happens, it brings socially disruptive consequences.

In strong contrast, the pastoralists display their feelings easily, openly, and seemingly "naturally." I assume that the emotions of pastoralists, like those of people anywhere, are subject to both conscious concealment and unconscious censorship; nevertheless, in comparison to farmers of the same tribe, pastoralists are remarkably expressive of a wide range of emotion. The good and the bad, the joyous and the sad, the soft and the harsh—all are expressed with far greater freedom. Perhaps because their feelings are so openly expressed, the pastoralists appear to lack those occasional impulsive lapses of control which occur among farmers.

Edgerton 1971:280–281.

We predicted that witchcraft would be more prevalent among the farmers than among the pastoralists because we see witchcraft as an instrument for the covert expression of suppressed hostility, which farmers had more need to repress than pastoralists. This is possible because pastoralists can walk away from disputes, taking their livelihood with them, which obviously farmers cannot do, and must therefore suppress their rage. We found that this was the case in three of the tribes, but not in the fourth. Three out of four does not offer very convincing support, but the anomaly was revealing. Witchcraft in the tribe that didn't conform to our prediction was overwhelmingly between husbands and wives. Since our hypothesis had rested on the assumption of the mobility of pastoralists, this would not have been operative with respect to spouses, who have little respectable opportunity to move apart. This gives some support for our belief that witchcraft tends to flourish when hostility is being suppressed.

A word of caution is called for here. These differences between the two life modes are real, significant, and far-reaching, but one must not think that either is better than the other. Each mode of economy made the best use of the environment that it could with the technological abilities their traditions had endowed them and suffered the difficulties inherent in the two lifestyles. Each is an adaptation to its own environment, and each mode of production makes its own demands on the people and offers its own special hazards; neither should be read as more primitive than the other in some kind of progressive evolutionary scale. The changes show the *evolutionary process* at work under natural conditions and without pressure from outside governments. It illustrates how environmental conditions call for specific production techniques, which in turn favor certain kinds of behavior and certain kinds of collaboration and call for their own institutional and cultural solutions. This is the model for the evolution of culture that we discuss in the next chapter.

Culture is a matrix for behavior, not a blueprint. Much of anthropological theory rests on the covert premise of cultural fixity in tribal societies; witness the prevalence of such ideas as the "cake of custom" and words like structure, stasis, and equilibrium rather than process, change, and adaptability. Extensive evidence to the contrary is written off as "acculturation." We get caught in our own myths. In the most stable of cultures, some men will resist taking part in these dramas or will rewrite the script to fit their own predilections. Colin Turnbull (1961) tells us about Cephu among the Ituri pygmies, whose hunting practices were so deplorable that the community was tempted to ostracize him, but he charmed the people with his story-telling. I got my lesson from Nablessa, a young man in the Sebei cattle-keeping area, while recording the extensive hearings on the estate of Kambuya, the richest man in the village of Kapsirika (1969). That event was a dramatic expression of personal agendas. The central plot was the conflict between two full brothers, with reciprocal accusations of witchcraft implicitly insinuating that the other had been having sex with their father's now deceased youngest wife and thus was "responsible" for their father's death. The hearings themselves became an item on the personal agenda of the elders, as expressed on the third day of the difficult decisions by one who said that they must be careful to do everything right "or else people will talk." There were enough subplots in these extended discussions of the relationships among Kambuya's heirs and neighbors to satisfy a Shakespearean scholar. Nablessa's father was one of the elders and insisted that one of Kambuya's cows belonged to his son—which Nablessa adamantly refused to take (like refusing GE stock in an uncle's will), to his father's outrage and to my surprise. I don't know what motivated this un-Sebei sentiment, but clearly he didn't want to play the cattle-numbers game, though it really was the only game in that pastoral town.

Summary

Culture makes possible the flexibility that is needed in order for humans to invade every niche on the earth's surface. It is more guide than blueprint, more ideal than guide. Early in this chapter I suggested that culture can be seen as cyberspace. Like all metaphors, it can be misleading. The cultural universe is a verbal creation, but it cannot entirely escape the physical reality that is out there and with which it must cope. In pragmatic matters it is tethered to the laws of thermodynamics. The feathered arrow does fly straighter than the plain one; the atomic bomb is more powerful than those made with TNT. Human beings show anger and lust even though they "know they shouldn't" and don't want to. Cyber-people *may* go into some eternity, but human bodies *always* die.

The symbolic selves that our collective imaginations have created over the millennia turn out to be potentially more fierce than
the tiger, more powerful than the elephant. The ancient urge to
propel the genes into the future by killing the prey and getting the
mate were neither tamed nor done away with, but harnessed
in the service of furthering the welfare of the symbolic self—and
let the genes be damned! The urge to do things differently, to do
them better, is not in the interest of one's own progeny, but in the
interest of the living self, and yet it has served the species well.
The evolutionary process brought us the seeds for this at the outset, but in the end it was our own doing. The interest in the symbolic self was a stronger motivation for accomplishment (and thus
for change) than any biological motivation, as the next chapter
shows.

7

Cultural Evolution

The flexibility in human behavior made it so adaptable that we could learn to occupy virtually every terrestrial environment on the globe. Once we got going, we did so with great rapidity. Consider the following: Twenty-five hundred years separate us from the classical age of Greece; double that (ca. 5,000 years ago) and you get to the earliest known states; double that (ca. 10,000 years ago) and you get to the first agriculture; double that (ca. 20,000 years) and you get to the great cave art of Europe; one more doubling (ca. 40,000 years) gets you to the first evidence of religious belief at the beginning of the Upper Paleolithic. This describes an exponential curve. But Homo sapiens was on the scene about four times as long before the start of this curve. That is why the Upper Paleolithic transition is sometimes called a "cultural explosion." This remarkable history is a product of *cultural* evolution.

The Nature of Cultural Evolution

Cultural evolution mimics biological evolution in being ecological (the dynamic relation between a community and the environment). But now the community that evolves is a society rather than a species. This evolution is driven by an increasingly efficient exploitation of resources, with human inventiveness replacing genetics to bring these changes. There is a natural selection for those that are better able to cope with the conditions, but the selection is for cultural knowledge instead of genes. The major difference, however, is that the innovations that constitute the driving force in this process are transmitted from one living person to another and therefore do not have to wait for generations of individual selection. This is Lamarck's "inheritance of acquired traits." It also has something of a purposive element, for humans can (and sometimes do) look to the future and seek solutions to problems.

I think no anthropologist today would doubt that this has been the history of our species, though when I entered the profession, the idea of cultural evolution that had been promoted in the 19th century had been rejected. This was because classical cultural evolution carried a subliminal elitist message based on ethnocentric values: "from apes to us [Western Europeans]." My thesis involves no value judgment other than survival value. My concern is in the dynamics of the adaptive change and the ultimate effect on human social behavior.

In both cultural and biological evolution there can be major breakthroughs, and one of these was the introduction of food production by planting crops and keeping food animals. Tribal peoples can be divided between the foragers, who are seen as people whose ancestors never went through this transition and therefore are seen to represent something like the ur-condition of humanity; the horticulturalists, who grow food with the use of digging stick or hoe; and pastoralists, who live on the products of their animals. Grain production, especially when abetted by harnessing animal labor for plowing, led to cities and state governments and what we call civilization. These technological differences are viewed as marking off "stages" of development, but the socially significant aspect of these economic innovations lies in the number of people they support. For instance, the rich resources of the fjords of the Northwest Coast supported populations as large as most that were sustained by horticulture and their cultures are as complex as many of them. Again, hoe farming in the lush areas of tropical Africa supported kingdoms that rivaled in population and social complexity the early states in the Near East. To paraphrase a saying about politics, "all ecology is local." For example, it is possible to make some generalizations about pastoralists, but the reindeer herders of the Asian Arctic, Yak herders of Tibet, sheep herders in the Near East, and Maasai of East Africa, all getting their basic livelihood by herding large animals, are more different in culture than alike.

There had to be a transition to culture before cultural evolution could take place—a gradual transition that took place over millions of years. We know that the upright posture goes back over three million years, which means the hands were freed, presumably to be used to handle things better than monkeys can, and that stone artifacts go back well over a million years; by the time we get to *Homo habilis* we have, as its name implies, an ancestor that is regularly making things. This means that a lot of evolution took place before Homo sapiens came on the scene. The modern world does not provide us with examples of the transitional forms of society any more than it does of partially developed languages, and we can only imagine what took place.

This Lower Paleolithic evolution must have started with the gradual spread of pre-*sapiens* hominids during which they found diverse ecological niches that could support them with adaptations that might be either location-specific or by means of increased behavioral flexibility that enabled them to make a "cultural adaptation." This must have led to a radiation into separate species or subspecies, in which ultimately those of our ancestors that chose the more flexible route could take over more and more ecological niches and ultimately push out those with more fixed adaptation until only our species remained. The last to go were the Neanderthal, if European data can be depended upon. Behavioral flexibility thus became the ultimate evolutionary advantage over our nearest ecological rivals as our ancestry eliminated the competition, taking over the final stages of the evolutionary process with their increasing cleverness. This explains why no other species of the genus *Homo* or even the family *Hominidae* exists today.[1] We

---

1. While I was preparing this manuscript for the printer, the *Los Angeles Times* reported the finding of *Homo floresiensis*, the three-foot hominids who adapted to island life by miniaturing themselves, as did the pachyderms there. This is encouraging support for my scenario of florescence and selection in the hominid line—as found in other evolutionary sequences.

can hardly deplore this savagery since we are still doing it to the apes, who deprive us only of very marginal resources, and, even more sadly, to less "successful" members of our own species.

Once Homo sapiens had covered the earth, cultural evolution could begin in earnest. Now *societies* became the unit of selection, competing with one another, as beehives do. In this process, the more "advanced" cultures eliminate ethnic entities but not necessarily their genomes, for conquered people usually are subordinated or enslaved and then marry or mate with their conquerors and so continue to contribute to the gene pool. (There is currently some debate as to whether this also happened with the Neanderthals.) At least, that is what usually happens now, despite repeated tragic but futile efforts at genocide. It must have been rough going in the beginning. Life could not have been easy for the early hominids surrounded by better-equipped predators that just knew how to do things and didn't have to learn them. I have a fantasy of a philosophical sort of hominid living several hundred millennia ago. She is sitting under a tree and wondering if all this business about learning was really worthwhile, since her life seems no better than that of the other animals. She could foresee neither the SSTs, Jags, PCs, and VCRs (nor SEC, atom bombs, or jails) in her future—nor that her progeny would come to dominate the planet. This scenario is not provable but it is more plausible than any other I know and is not contradicted by any scientific data now available. We must remember that the data are very sketchy; it is not only that the samples are very small but also that they are not random, limited as they are to only the least perishable items from environments that are least destructive and most available to exploration.

The Search for Eden

Anthropologists have tried to describe the original human society ever since anthropology began, using modern "primitives" as the model. Early explanatory efforts argued over the precedence of matriliny or patriliny, fuelling the battle of the sexes more than contributing to human history. This fool's errand lingers on, showing up in current discussions of sexual behavior and dietary preferences[2] as having evolved by adapting to the conditions of some imagined aboriginal Eden. It goes along with the announcement of having found the evolutionary Eve. To ask the obvious question, "and what about her mother?" exposes the fallacy in this kind of evolutionary perception. It is an example of the linguistic need to make discrete entities out of a process that leads to this falsification.

The quest for this ur-society has led to looking for examples among contemporary foragers. They give a murky window even to the Upper Paleolithic because the societies that initiated the Neolithic could push the "backward" foragers off such lands as were amenable to cultivation, leaving them in the marginal areas where some have remained until now, to be available for ethnographic study. The natural tendency is to examine the simplest of these, that is, the poorest in resources—the very ones that are *not* a sample of pre-Neolithic foragers. Furthermore, despite the common poverty in resources, these marginal-land foragers vary widely in culture. The Australian aborigines living in the arid outback have a highly formalized social system with strict gerontocratic control, elaborate marriage rules, and age-grades marked off by a series of initiations that gradually lift the restrictions controlling the younger men. The Mbuti, who live in the Ituri forest in the Congo River basin in Africa, have very few marital and behavioral restrictions, build no large kin structures; they also allow youths to raise issues in public. One can even see the differences in cultural tonus by looking at pictures of them if one is sensitive to body language. (The Aranda/Mbuti contrast is shown in Sidebar 13.)

Which to choose? The claim each can make to represent the earliest society is impaired for every forager society in one way or another. The Mbuti have symbiotic relations with Neolithic farmers; the San have borrowed the use of iron for arrowheads from their neighbors; the Inuit live in a very specialized environment. Some modern foragers seem to have once been cultivators. The

---

2. The dietary preference must have been catholic, or else Homo sapiens would not have evolved with an omnivorous digestive system.

DIVERSITY IN FORAGER SOCIAL STRUCTURE AND ETHOS

	Aranda	*Mbuti*
Sexual division of work	Men hunt large game; women and children hunt small game and gather plant foods. Women do all domestic chores and care for children. Dry season separation into domestic units.	Men hunt; women gather plants, insects, lizards and shellfish; fishing is women's work where it occurs. Men share domestic chores and care of small children. Where nets used, men and women cooperate in hunting.
Band organization	The group sharing a territory is not clearly defined in sources available.	The band of several domestic units is basic social unit, sharing a territory and its resources, reinforced by band rituals.
Social structure	Marriage classes define who may get married, while totemic clans (and sex and age distinctions) dominate all other social interactions.	No structural feature other than bands.
Age distinctions	Rituals mark off age distinctions for males, starting at age ca. eight and continuing well into adulthood, as determined by elders. Activities and social participation determined by age status.	No formalized distinction by age and even youths, as well as women, may raise issues in public.

Marital rules and arrangements	Must marry spouse in established marital class. Arrangements made by fathers of principles. (Sex outside is incest but rules allow for breaches.)	Sibling and first cousin marriage forbidden and most wives move to husband's band. Choice of spouse up to principles in marriages.
Kinship	Kinship system is highly complex; it universalizes role relationships, creating demanded or expected forms of social interaction between all dyadic pairs, in conformity with putative kinship.	Kinship system plays a minor role in dyadic relationships.
Social control	Authority is age and sex based. Old men who have undergone all initiations have sole access to the spirit world. They have been selected not only on basis of age but also on their conformity to social rules and esoteric knowledge.	Social control is by consensus; any man, woman, or youth can bring complaint before village. Chief sanction available against misbehavior is ostracism, reluctantly applied.
Ritual	Rituals reinforce clan strength (although clans are not local bands) and individual social advancement. All the latter involve pain to the initiate, ranging from whipping of eight-year-olds to subincision.	Major rituals reinforce band unity. None cause physical pain.

Aranda: Spencer and Gillen 1927; Mbuti: Turnbull, 1961, 1965.

Tasmanians were the most cut off from advancements and had the least sophisticated technology, but they had environmental limitations—and anyway were killed off before much was learned about their culture. The least "contaminated" are the Australian aborigines, but their lands are extremely harsh and their customs and mythic world are so sophisticated that they look like remnants of a larger and richer forager society. The environmental conditions of the Australian Outback, the Arctic, the Kalahari, or the Congo are not likely to characterize those in which Paleolithic society was forged.

Only one part of the world was not "contaminated" by outside cultural contributions or the pressures of a technologically superior Neolithic people. This is the western slope of North America. Much of this area was fully amenable to cultivation and animal husbandry, as subsequent history has shown, yet it was occupied by foragers when first encountered by the sweep of history. Some must have known about farming, for they traded with farming people. Nascent farming apparently did not tempt them to cultivate lands that were so rich in wild grasses, acorns, game, and fish. When we look to them for a model of Paleolithic social life we are in even greater trouble. The lands extending from the semi-arid peneplane of southern California northward to the rich fjords and rain forests of British Columbia and southeast Alaska and eastward to the tundra of Canada and the Rockies and the deserts of the American West offer a wide array of economic opportunities. The Shoshone of the Great Basin have as simple a social organization as any known, while those of the fertile and teeming fjords of Alaska and British Columbia are among the richest and most elaborate tribal cultures known to ethnography.

Ironically, this does suggest what conditions were like in the Upper Paleolithic, but it is no satisfaction to those hunting for *the* model of early human society, for *variation itself is the model.* By the time our species came into existence and had spread throughout the world, it had acquired the tools and the behavioral adaptability to take advantage of all the diverse conditions it found. Consider the great expanse of the Paleolithic world, extending from the tropics to the Arctic, from seashore to mountain and from desert to forest. Then expand this universe further to include changes (with glacial advances and retreats) that took place over a hundred or more millennia, during which Homo sapiens lived before they left evidence for what we call the Upper Paleolithic. The conquest of these diverse areas, offering different resources and hazards, was achieved by making technical and social adaptations to the conditions that each presented. There is not one model for Paleolithic society; there is a model of ecological adaptability. The Upper Paleolithic had diverse cultures.

Ecological Adaptations

We cannot use modern primitive societies as models of Paleolithic ones, but we can use ethnographic data to show us the social results of ecological adaptation under diverse environmental conditions. We have seen how the pastoral/farming shift involved adaptive changes in the kind of work and defense their respective ecologies demanded and how, in turn, these changes influenced other aspects of the social relations and raised new social problems for which new solutions were needed. The process like the one we saw at work in East Africa must have taken place over and over again in human history. The chain of causal relationship goes like this: Technology advances productivity → greater productivity increases population → population growth makes for larger social units → larger social units complicate the problem of maintaining order → these problems require institutional adjustments. Finally, because we must look at social systems from the standpoint of the individual, we must see how different adaptations handle the universal need for affect and a sense of self. We are interested in how the institutions of interpersonal relations changed with differing levels of ecology and how they affected individuals.

The only viable generalization about how the simplest known societies live is that they recognize something we might call a family unit—a man and one or more women and their children. These always see themselves as part of a named unit (a band) of some 20 persons who share a more-or-less clearly delineated territory and interact on a daily basis. (Under some conditions, such households may spend most of the year separated from one another.) Such bands, in turn, always recognize themselves as part of a more inclusive named group of several such bands with whom they interact, intermarry, and may either collaborate or fight—or both. There are rules of descent and marriage among people at this simplest stage of organization, but they are not consistent other than that all forbid close kin to marry. Even then, they do not all define close kin the same way. They have one other common institution: "kinship systems." But then, every society has this social feature. Anthropologists from the very beginning have known this and have tried to study why they vary so widely but have neglected even to think about the singular fact that having them is perhaps the only truly universal institution designed to define how people are expected to fit together. That is what we will focus on.

Belonging and the Self: Kinship

Every society takes cognizance of the way its members are related to one another by descent and marriage and uses special terms for classes of such kin. They are words for people, and we already know that words always create categories. The words that are used by the speakers always refer to persons and yet kinship systems are not taxonomies of people, but of *relationships*. For instance, we call the man who sired us "father" and his brother "uncle." We call our mother's brother "uncle" too, and we are expected to treat these uncles alike and expect that they will all have the same general behavior toward us. In many tribal societies, this is not the case; the father's brothers are called father but the mother's brother something different and the father and his brothers are treated as being the same. There is no confusion about paternity, for the criterion is about behavioral expectation. So the kinterm really refers to the relationship, not the persons. Why are kinship systems universal?

Every infant in tribal societies grows up in immediate contact with his mother, father, and siblings, and kinship systems expand the dyadic relationships of this domestic ménage outward into the community to engulf everyone, extrapolating the experiences of infancy to the ever-widening relationships in the community. In small-scale tribal societies this may literally include every person with whom a person comes in contact except strangers (often defined as "enemies"). A kinship system can in this way define the appropriate behavior and feeling toward each person with whom he or she brings to every social encounter. We by now know that not all people always live by all the rules, but in tribal societies kinship systems offer an orderly network of expectations, at least. Needless to say, both the categories and the appropriate behavior differ from one culture to another. A society is thus a web of kindred, which is to say, a web of meaningful predefined social relationships. Every person throughout life knows who he is and where he stands. This makes for an orderly template for social interaction; it also goes a long way toward defining the self.

These simple observations are what really matter, but attention has focused on how and why they vary and most have focused on incest and marriage and the historic precedence of male versus female descent. There are a few interesting correlates to kin behavior: A high correlation is seen between pastoral economies and patrilineal descent; peasant villages are usually patrilineal; and most matrilineal societies are horticulturalists but not all horticulturalists are matrilineal. These are not correlations that shed light on forager societies and so cannot illuminate that chimera of an Eden.

Kinship systems extend the feelings laid down in the bosom of the family, building on the experiences each member of the family had at the outset of his life. This single pan-human *cultural* feature is a product of the *biologically requisite* affective encounter that each newborn human has; their affective quality of this encounter is captured and given permanence by the language in which it was learned. The first word every child learns is the word for mother and then for others in the natal environment. Structuring social relations starts there, whether in the Australian outback or a Park Avenue penthouse, whether in the end it has the warmth we idealize or the misery it can have. We apparently have an inherent capacity for bonding, creating an emotional tonus between the neonate and his immediate social environment that gets attached to the words as well as the human referent, extending the expected sentiments to all belonging to that category, whether it be the mother who had nurtured or the cousin of the sort that is expected to become a spouse.

Clans

The system of codified one-on-one relationships can serve very well to keep order in communities of 20 or so persons, but it has size limitations. It can be expanded into what appears to be the second oldest means of organizing society, the formalization of kindred into groups, usually called clans. Clan membership is inherited and is treated as family even when it has grown so large that the genealogy that links members together is largely fictional. Being family, they cannot marry one another, and so every person has a parent of another clan; that is, clans are exogamous and have to intermarry and there must be more than one in any society. Thus clans are an artificial extension of the systematic aspect of kinship. The clan system appears to be very old; it is widespread, has shown remarkable staying power, and gives evidence of having been invented more than once. In summary, clans have the following traits: (1) They are a named and recognized group of people who constitute one part of a larger society that is made up of a number of such groups; (2) membership is consistently determined on the basis of genealogy, either on the mother's side (matriliny) or the father's (patriliny); (3) members are seen as a family and must not marry one another (exogamy) but choose a spouse from another clan; (4) clan membership is automatic according to established rules, universal among the tribe, and eternal; and (5) clan bonds are deeply embedded in the psyches of their members, whether or not they have the religious reinforcement of totemism.

While clans always control the rules of marriage and descent, they also often perform one or more other functions: (1) They serve as a unit in a legal sense so that each is responsible for the actions of all; (2) they own land or other resources, with each household having access to it or to its fruits; (3) they celebrate rituals to reinforce the belief in their spiritual unity with their ancestors and their symbolic totem (totemism); and (4) they extend beyond the local community to unify larger areas of common culture.

Most of the poorest and impoverished societies do not have clans, but some do. The Native Americans in central California did not have clans though the population seems large, dense, and stable enough to warrant them and they did seem to be on the threshold of having them. They lacked the unifying element provided by religious belief and there seemed not to have been sufficient external threat to provoke such unification (Goldschmidt 1948). You will recall that the Hupa and Yurok did not have clans but had created a substitute with the ritually reinforced transient alliances made public at the Deerskin Dance. That these transient alliances did not offer as secure a haven as clans may be seen as having brought on those dramatic and tense expressions of individuation that we saw.

I had two field experiences that illustrate the strong hold that clans can have on their members. Studying the sensitive subject of land rights among the matrilineal Tlingit, we went from village to village; the first question asked of our interpreter in each was: "Who is your mother?" His clan's high standing made the rest easy for us. The second instance was more dramatic. It occurred among the patrilineal Sebei, whose clans usually settle legal disputes either by jointly paying compensation or by feuding; they also have a third method, which is to make ritualized oaths that were quasi-legal acts of witchcraft. These oaths work by killing *any* member of the accused clan, and this practice has a built-in deterrent: If the accusation is false, the oath turns upon the one who made it and kills *any* member of his clan. When an old man from the cattle-keeping sector threatened such an oath against a neighbor he was accusing of having twice abetted the theft of his cattle, his young clansmen heard him and became wild-eyed with fury. Shaking with fear and anger, they said, "You are old and ready to die, but what will happen to us?" The strength of their feeling astonished me, for the Sebei pay much less attention to their clans than to the age-sets formed by their initiations. But whether they really cared about their clansmen, they were a part of it and so knew who they were, even if it was not always advantageous.

Clans often morph into chieftaincies when populations grow still larger. One clan sets itself up as a "royal" clan with appropriate mythical justification and takes over the role of governance, establishing tribunals to settle disputes among the clans, in lieu of the clan-to-clan justice of direct confrontation. An external threat created by the Arab slave trade inspired the Shambala in what is now Tanzania to make this shift early in the 19th century. One of the clans asserted its "royal" standing and took power over the other, but its authority seemed tenuous and it had to buy the loyalty of the others by curbing its own powers (Winans 1962). Something of the kind took place centuries earlier among the Baganda, whose powerful empire we discussed earlier. The Kabaka's totalitarian authority was based on mythical action that named its clan as descendant of the sun and built a large army, an elaborate bureaucracy, and a priesthood that enforced Draconian powers to protect itself from the power of the other clans. Yet they also gave other clans social and ritual functions to get their loyalty. Clans also persisted in peasant rural China over centuries of national statehood. Urban Chinese paid little attention to clan affiliation, as the demand for reciprocity that characterizes clan membership leads peasants to make claims on urban salaried people, which they cannot reciprocate.

Human society has used the sentiments of the nursery to shape and order community social relationships. It makes no sense to see this as a continuation of some specific animal precursor, for cultures have bent and stretched whatever went into the animal origin to fit their diverse needs as their worlds altered in the evolutionary process. But it is appropriate to recognize its animal origin in kin bonding as being inherent proclivities that are being culturally reshaped. Though it is impossible to demonstrate that the clan was the first artificially defined social entity to come into being, it strikes me as reasonable and likely. Clans have been supplemented by other organizations: age-sets as among the Sebei, military societies with much the same purpose on the American Plains, religious fraternities among the Pueblo Indians, and ad hoc entities such as those among the Yurok and Hupa—or by none other than the local settlement, as in central California. No other system has been repeatedly invented or has shown such staying power. This suggests that they are not just a pragmatic solution to problems of social control, but perform a useful psychological function—to give individuals a vital sense of belonging, a haven of comfort in the search for that nurturance that had been so comforting in infancy. Freud called this womb envy, but this is more figure of speech than analysis. Evolutionary psychologists will see this phenomenon as the workings of parent–child bonding, and I have no quarrel with this if it is recognized that this *biological* mechanism results in attachments that are made according to *cultural* directives. (Note: The bonding to the clan was just as strong among the patrilineal Sebei as among the matrilineal Tlingit.)

Urban Transformations

The city came into being with the emergence of a technological proficiency that produced enough of the necessities of life to enable people to be specialists, exchanging what they create for these necessities. Like foraging and pastoralism, it is an ecological category with like demographic problems but with diverse specific solutions. They always involve some system of governance and some means of marketing goods so the essential exchange of goods and services can take place. Cities have always been made up by the in-migration of people from the peasant hinterland villages or nearby tribes. The earliest urban sites show that all the immigrants from one place congregate in local neighborhoods, making the city a mosaic of cultures, each retaining much of its past customs but gradually melting into the urban whole as generations of children intermarry. This multiculturalism is an inevitable product of urban life. Living cheek by jowl with peoples of diverse culture and occupational lifestyle means that traditions can no longer be the basis for all interpersonal relationships. Therefore rules must be formalized and enforced by some established authority. The Code of Hamurabi is the best known among the early efforts to formulate the "law of contract" as distinct from the "law of status," which characterizes legal action among members of tribal societies, as Sir Henry Maine (1963) called the distinction between promulgated law and traditional rules, respectively.

The conditions of urban life raise problems not only in the maintenance of order but also in the individual's search for affect and for a sense of self. In tribal life, both how one should act and whose opinions matter are clear and uniform, but urban multiculturalism and depersonalization create a pervasive confusion of social directives. The template for measurement is obscured both by the diversity of cultural values and by the blurred audience whose judgment is to be respected. At the close of the chapter on affect hunger I noted that there were basically two ways to satisfy it: by belonging and by performance. Urban life, with its occupational specialization and the weakening of traditional social unities, tilts this choice in favor of performance, and the peer group whose judgment is valued is constituted increasingly of occupational colleagues.

The opening of the New World inspired a giant diaspora from Europe, breaking local and family ties. The hunger for belonging was intensified among émigrés who left both family and village to come to America. Alexis de Tocqueville describes the newly settled pioneers' propensity for joining societies of various kinds when he visited America in the 1830s, showing that these uprooted people needed to belong to something, even if they had to create it themselves. Sometimes the hunger is expressed in terminology, as when both labor unions and the new "Lodges" and "Fraternities" use the idiom of kinship in addressing fellow members. The Japanese, whose industrialization has led to similar loss of the sense of belonging, have met the issue in their corporate culture, adapting old traditions by treating the corporation as family, with the mutual obligations this implies and the problems that it can bring to both management and labor.

Just as the people who came to the first cities at the dawn of the Neolithic settled into ethnic neighborhoods, so did those who came to America. Ethnicity became a major dynamic in the American culture. Ethnic ties are an even more diluted version of biology than clans are, but they appeal to these family-based sentiments that seem to lie deep within us. The intensified interest in ethnic background at the present time is a manifestation of this hunger for belonging. This also applies to the resurgence of fundamentalist religion that is happening everywhere in the modern world. Such quasi-traditional groups also give guidelines to behavior in this world of confused values. The nationalization of the American economy in the 20th century increased both the physical and the social mobility, further reducing the sense of place and of belonging as children regularly moved to new pastures and hundreds of communities literally disappeared. None of the diverse kinds of belonging now seems quite as potent as the workplace, job, or profession as the matrix for the self. Like the Sebei pastoralists, we seem to take our social base and economic resources that give us our sense of self with us as we wander from place to place seeking opportunity.

Possessions and the Self

We have seen that possessions play a big role in defining who a person is among tribal peoples. They can take on a spiritual quality, as shown by the Hupa and Yurok dance paraphernalia, and even represent the personal spirits, as with the Aranda churingas. They take on an even greater, if less personal, role in the modern world, where the tokens of expression of personal value are measured in that antiseptic medium, money, and in the depersonalized public arena of modern life. This, together with the narrowing and weakening of family ties, deprives an ever-growing sector of the population of the more direct physical expressions of affect. Money is the most fungible of status symbols and therefore the most mobile. It is also the least personal and often becomes an end in itself, as shown by the regular evaluation of sports and entertainment stars, corporate CEOs, movies, and even artistic masterpieces by the money they rake in. The ratings of athletes seems to be much the same as the rating of CEOs—annual cash income—so that one does not know whether we are looking at the financial or sports section of the paper. Protestant theology fostered individualism by seeing the wealthy as having validated their state of grace by their success, with the ultimate consequence of giving to money a spirituality like that of the Yurok and Hupa.

This intensified self-interest disregards the community. While community can be disregarded, it cannot be denied. In the first place, nobody's success is a purely individual accomplishment, for all things of significance involve input from many people. This removal of affect reward from its original evolutionary function of inducing individuals to serve the needs of the community comes at a great cost to social life. Making social rewards ends in themselves rather than a reflection of service to the public leads to the excesses of an affluent society given to the pursuit of the conspicuous consumption that Thorstein Veblen called to our attention in his classic, *The Theory of the Leisure Class,* at the close of the 19th century (1899). He had been influenced by Franz Boas's description of the Kwakiutl excesses of the potlatch, and it amuses me to realize that the Northwest Coast Indians elite were profiting from the same chain of fur trade that filled the Victorian parlors in New England, each indulging in conspicuous waste in their pursuit of symbolic affect.

Arête

Most societies give expression to a kind of generalized conception of the attributes a good person should be endowed with, a concept that recognizes a commitment to community values and a purposeful pursuit of them. As usual, the Greeks had a word for this: arête. It is a word that defies easy translation, and it is perhaps for that reason that it has not taken hold in the Western World. It means the quality of a person who has internalized the values of his culture, who has the capacity to fulfill them in all areas of life, so that it has echoes of the concept of the "Renaissance Man" as well as the German expression, "das ist ein Mensch." The actual content will vary with the culture, for what constitutes the centrality of valued knowledge, capability, and propriety are culturally determined. In classic Greek society it placed as much emphasis on athletics as on philosophical and military prowess, as Stephen Miller's recent book, *Arete: Greek Sports from Ancient Sources* (2004), makes clear. The word stems from early Greek culture where it embodied the values of a more militant tribal culture, but later, it took on the philosophical and aesthetic qualities of the slave-holding gentility who dominated the "golden age of Greece." The anthropologists have always concerned themselves with these variants, and we have seen how propriety differs between the Zuni gentle self-effacement and Kwakiutl social aggression, as well as between the Yurok and Hupa aggressive, haughty self-interest and Baganda sycophancy. As one moves from one culture region to another, one can see the variant dominant moods expressed in single words or phrases that express the essential content of the respective arête: "face" among the Chinese, "honor" in the Balkans and throughout the Arab world, "earned merit" in Hindu-dominated lands, "faith" in Catholic countries, "independence" in the traditions of northern Europe and America, and the like. These are, of course, ideals as well as generalities, but they do tend to give a kind of standard against which to measure the self. The monetary standard for social standing in the industrial world obscures the behavioral demands, for the social value of money is independent of the manner in which it was obtained.

Affect Deprivation

The most privileged in our society, those who would seem to have a surfeit, continue the quest for more with an unabated determination that seems obsessive. Though we all spend much of our energy throughout life in the pursuit of symbolic rewards, I believe that in the end they are not fully satisfying. However much we revel in the sense of who we are, at the end of the day, we want the warmth of friends and family. Our pursuit reminds me of those dreams I have had in which I am fiendishly thirsty and drink glass after glass of refreshing liquids that never slake my thirst. The evolutionary advantage of affect hunger lay in its ability to induce the individual to be committed to his community— to be a socially responsible person. But it did this by giving humans an internal *physiological need*. Thus it is that the physiological hunger seems to continue to gnaw at us, the rewards in symbolic form failing to satisfy these physical desires. Affect responses must, so to speak, gratify both the body and the soul—and to this we turn next.

8

Body and Soul

Before closing, we need to revisit some philosophical issues that this book has raised but I have glossed over. We begin by examining what "reality" means. I have assiduously avoided treating cultural constructs as having less reality than matters with a tangible, visible physical presence. I have done so because in the world as it is lived in everyday life cultural constructs are not seen as separate matters and certainly are not dealt with differently in normal discourse. Nor do they have less effect on our lives. Furthermore, all significant elements in the more physical parts of the environment are so encrusted with cultural meanings that the distinction between the physical and the constructed realities is blurred. Nevertheless, they are ontologically different, for the cultural constructs do not have to obey the laws of physics. An infinity of angels *can* dwell on the head of a pin, and, by the same token, the mind (what the brain does) can share the same space in the skull as the brain because it has no separate materiality. So we must spend some time looking at this broader antithesis before we can deal with that classical philosophical dichotomy between body and soul.

The Ontology of Reality

I am not about to try to tell you what reality really is, but it is fair to look at how we come to think things are real. The ecology of the mind has changed as technicians and technology have enabled us to discover aspects of the physical world that were formerly unavailable, and this has undermined the mythic reality of earlier generations. Our telescopes have penetrated farther into space and our microscopes deeper into matter with all kinds of surprising results. When I was in college, I was told that the gene could never be seen because it was smaller than the wavelength of light, but before I graduated, the electron microscope had changed all that. And space turns out to be filled with more physical realities that boggle the mind to displace those of the imagination.

We apprehend the real world with our senses; the things we feel, see, hear, and so on are what we think of as real. It was difficult to convince persons experimenting with hallucinogens that what they had seen did not exist, just as it is impossible to convince anyone who has "seen" monsters or ghosts, whether out of psychopathy or religious conviction, that they are not real. Our senses are limited, and there are many manifestations of external reality that we have learned to know about because scientific instruments have translated them into modalities that we can perceive. We bring such things into our world of "reality" when the evidence of their existence seems clear. There are other things out there that science has not brought into the orbit of our sense faculties which we also accept as physically real, such as gravity, because we perceive its manifestations. So even the physical world is not always "real" in the sense we normally use the word.

Some assessments of what is real rest entirely on belief. The beliefs of others, whether tribal peoples or our own ancestors, can seem charming, imaginative, fantastic, foolish, or misbegotten, depending on how they appeal to us. Beliefs can be readily dismissed as things of the imagination. Those that we support, that are part of our cosmology, however, are another matter. Believing can actually bring about physical changes. There is a phenomenon prevalent in many cultures called "spirit possession," in which spirits are thought to have entered into the body; this involves an altered state of consciousness that can affect the autonomous physiological functions of the body. A most dramatic example is reported from Bali, where young maidens in religious ecstasy push sharp daggers into their bare breasts without bleeding. The more secular form of this phenomenon, called the "self-fulfilling prophecy," is in fact essential to the very existence of culture for, as indicated in earlier discussions, society depends on social consensus. When a population acts on the assumption that something is real, it gives experiential evidence of its reality. The nations of today owe their existence to belief and will disappear when their reality is no longer recognized by the public, just as have the British Empire and the empire of the USSR that dominated my high school atlas. Money loses its value when faith in its guarantors is lost. The banking community at present seems to have more fear that the public will lose trust (not believe) in the market as a result of the recent scandals than concern over the tragedies they caused—with doubtful morality but not without practical reason.

Language, too, rests on consensus. We accept that a word stands for something that is itself an entity and are upset when someone says, "it depends on what you mean by _____." A generation ago *Webster's Third International Dictionary* caused a furor in the legal community by offering relativistic definitions that were impossible to use in legal cases. The law needs concepts that are explicit and unchanging. This is not the nature of words, as words are inherently malleable. All languages create categories, and these may be misleading. I have examined a number of such misleading terms, notably the word "love" and the concept of "communication." The Linnaean classification of life-forms has greater validity for scientists than its predecessors because it is built on the basis of biological relatedness as products of evolution. It replaced the earlier classification by habitat (land, air, water), which might have been more useful to foragers. This example shows that the essence of a valid taxonomy lies in the features that are used as criteria and their relevance to what needs to be understood. We also saw this earlier with the classifications of race and of sex.

Whatever reality may be, we must recognize that there are two classes, one constituted of those things that are directly available to our senses and are part of the physical world and those things that are only perceived in our minds either because we have imagined them or because their existence has been validated for us by our having experienced their effects. With this in mind, I want to turn this discussion to the most central element in the dichotomy, directly related to the thesis being developed in this book: body and soul, or, in a more mundane form, genes and culture.

Body

Our physical being comes to each of us as a package of potentials. These potentials are preprogrammed for us and will be activated with the passage of time. Along the way these potentials are affected by the experiences of the individual so that what the ultimate manifestation will often, and perhaps always, be is the result of both the genetic programming and these environmental influences. We may take the learning of language as the prototype, for there is no reasonable doubt that we inherit the capacity for learning grammar and no doubt whatsoever that the grammar we learn depends on the grammar we hear. It can be said that every physical feature and every form of behavior that is engaged in by every normal person is both anticipated in the genetic code and influenced by social or environmental factors. This we have always known about physical features, and there is every reason to believe that behavioral characteristics have even greater plasticity.

Explanation is part of every culturally constructed world. Explaining what causes human behavior, whether in matters of physical health or acts of good and evil, has long been the province of superstition, religion, and theology. The Enlightenment brought much of this world of behavior into the realm of the rational system of understanding. This rationality has gradually expanded as scientists developed the tools that enabled them to see more deeply into physical matter and could effectively explain what causes such enigmatic matters as diseases. For instance, the "evil air" of gases emanating from swamps, from which malaria got its name, was not the cause of the disease, but the swamps were the breeding ground for the mosquitoes that transmit the disease vectors. Ludwik Fleck (1979), examining the history of explanations of syphilis from a carnal scourge to spirochete, summarizes his findings by saying that religious societies see it as punishment for fornication; astrological fraternities see it as action of the stars, medical personnel as "humors" of the blood, and early explanations as putting the onus on a "disease demon." The idea of some kind of divine retribution was quickly applied to AIDS when it was originally thought to be a malady of homosexuals. The frequent explanations for mishaps and personal losses found among tribal peoples is witchcraft. That was implicit in the query by a Sebei friend; when he learned about the disastrous fire in my home, he leaned over conspiratorially to ask, "*Who* caused your fire?"

We live in an era of scientific explanations and so in the popular mind, the "cause" must fit into a scientific paradigm. With respect to diseases, this usually invokes either genes, microorganisms, or both. There are difficulties with the causal models we work with, for not everyone who is exposed to a disease vector gets infected nor does everyone who is infected get the disease, as is the case with HIV-positive people and AIDS. Scientists and doctors are aware of this and for this reason make double-blind tests of the effectiveness of their cure by the use of placebos. The placebo phenomenon is itself of interest because it is a tacit recognition of inadequate knowledge of causation and, more important to our discussion, is a recognition of social factors as potentially contributing to the cause.

The 20th century has been called the century of the gene; Mendel's findings were rediscovered just as it began, and the Human Genome Project reported its findings just as it closed. I had hoped that the Human Genome Project would at least begin to tell us just what the limits are to what can be said to be "in our genes." The project advertised itself as having "decoded" the human genome when it really just encoded what its chemical components are and not what each gene actually does. It did what the French soldiers did in *finding* the Rosetta stone, not what Champollion did when he *translated* what the Egyptians were writing about. It gave us information on some isolated mental disorders but nothing that illuminates human behavior. Mendel initiated genetics by looking at the *inheritance of variability*, which the Human Genome Project was not even designed to look at. When I was in college the whole emphasis in genetics was on individual traits and the fact that there were two or more "alleles," parallel genes occupying the same location on the paired genes, each coming from a different parent and each contributing to the final outcome—that is, the "phenotype," as distinct from the "genotype."

The two might be the same or different; the latter might blend in some manner, as is the case with the sickle-cell anemia gene in humans; or one might be "dominant" over the other, thus continuing the phenotype. Such situations created variance within the population of a species, forming the ratios that led Mendel to see how the color of four o'clock blossoms, for instance, were transmitted. It was such genes that my teacher, Herman Muller, had mutated on drosophila with X rays, a revolutionary finding that won him the Nobel Laureate. Thus, at the time, there was a kind of subliminal notion that each gene produced a single trait and that each trait would have its own set of genetic alleles, if it had variable expressions in the species. I must confess that this formulation staggered my mind; it seemed like a kind of scientific version of how many angels can sit on the head of a pin. But I thought that if there can be billions of suns and billions of cells in our bodies and billions of synapses in our brains, then why shouldn't there be billions of genes?

But it turns out that there are only 20,000–25,000 genes in the human genome, according to the latest estimate based on a refinement of the sequencing as it had been reported in 2000 (Stein 2004). We had long known that the number of genes was not the astronomical figure I had imagined and that the one-gene-one-trait paradigm was not tenable. In fact, the geneticists had already moved on to a new level of analysis, called "epigenetics" (Gibbs 2003). The old trait formulation has been abandoned for a new, as yet not fully understood, form of multigene operation. "No single gene determines a particular behavior. Behaviors are complex traits involving multiple genes that are affected by a variety of other factors," according to a recent website report on behavioral genetics, which also points out that this is "a reality that complicates the search for genetic contributions" (McInerney and Rothstein 2004). It goes on to condemn the facile treatment of genetics in public discourse (see Sidebar 14). Those who are still devoted to biological determinism and are unaware of this 21st-century genetics and its recognition of genetic malleability are out of the loop. It is tempting to suggest that this apparent fluidity of gene expression among humans helps in bringing about the greater flexibility in human behavior and that the relatively fewer gene functions are

A CAUTIONARY NOTE ON THE GENETICS OF BEHAVIOR

A growing scientific and popular focus on genes and behavior has contributed to a resurgence of behavioral genetic determinism. Are behaviors inbred, written indelibly in our genes as immutable biological imperatives, or is the environment more important in shaping our thoughts and actions? Such questions cycle through society repeatedly, forming the public nexus of the "nature vs. nurture controversy," a strange locution to biologists, who recognize that behaviors exist only in the context of environmental influence. Nonetheless, the debate flares anew every few years, reigniting in response to genetic analyses of traits such as intelligence, criminality, or homosexuality, characteristics freighted with social, political, and legal meaning.

What social consequences would genetic diagnoses of such traits as intelligence, criminality, or homosexuality have on society? What effect would the discovery of a behavioral trait associated with increased criminal activity have on our legal system? If we find a "gay gene," will it mean greater or lesser tolerance? Will it lead to proposals that those affected by the "disorder" should undergo treatment to be "cured" and that measures should be taken to prevent the birth of other individuals so afflicted?

Much current research on genes and behavior also engenders very strong feelings because of the potential social and political consequences of accepting these supposed truths. Thus, more than any other aspect of genetics, discoveries in behavioral genetics should not be viewed as irrefutable until there has been substantial scientific corroboration.

No single gene determines a particular behavior. Behaviors are complex traits involving multiple genes that are affected by a variety of other factors. This fact often gets overlooked in media reports hyping scientific breakthroughs on gene function, and, unfortunately, this can be very misleading to the public. For example, a study published in 1999 claimed that overexpression of a particular gene in mice led to enhanced learning capacity. The popular press referred to this gene as "the learning gene" or the "smart gene." What the press didn't mention was that the learning enhancements observed in this study were short-term, lasting only a few hours to a few days in some cases. Dubbing a gene as a "smart gene" gives the public a false impression of how much scientists really know about the genetics of a complex trait like intelligence.

> With disorders, behaviors, or any physical trait, genes are just a part of the story, because a variety of genetic and environmental factors are involved in the development of any trait. Having a genetic variant doesn't necessarily mean that a particular trait will develop. The presence of certain genetic factors can enhance or repress other genetic factors. Genes are turned on and off, and other factors may be keeping a gene from being turned "on." In addition, the protein encoded by a gene can be modified in ways that can affect its ability to carry out its normal cellular function.
>
> McInerney and Rothstein 2004.

made possible by the substitution of the cultural (i.e., learned) information, but it is not in my competence to do more than call attention to the possibility. The paradigm has shifted, and to say "there must be a gene for it" is as out of date as saying that "it is in our blood."

The taxonomy of the primates is much disputed, and I feel it often involves a hidden agenda. Placing Neanderthals in our species seemed to me a kind of misplaced anti-racism, not wishing to stigmatize these extinct hominids. I never believed it, for if Homo sapiens and Neanderthals could have interbred, which is the defining feature of the concept of species, the separation of the two would have disappeared over the many millennia that they lived in the same part of the world. I also have similar misgivings about efforts to place the gorilla and chimpanzee in our genus in contrast to the classic taxonomy in *Walker's Mammals of the World,* which not only places Homo sapiens in its own genus, but also in its own family (Nowak and Paradiso 1983). It seems to me that this lumping disregards too great a differentiation in lifestyles and capabilities, depending on gene frequency data, which, as we have just seen, is still poorly understood. Our uniqueness as human beings is not a denial of our continuity with all other living things. Our uniqueness rests on our adaptability, which enabled us to occupy all the places for an animal like us, and it is inconceivable that any other species will ever challenge us. Indeed, further speciation of the genus *Homo* is impossible because we killed off all previously existing candidates, have occupied all the ecological niches useful to a large mammal, and now have a worldwide gene pool, making it impossible to isolate populations long enough for new varieties to develop.

Another and more interesting reason that it is impossible to have us evolve is the question of what version of modern man would be selected. I don't refer to which race, as appears to have been the presupposition of eugenicists, but what kind of special abilities or talents. For the very humanitarianism of human beings works against the process of natural selection by keeping alive people who could not survive without help, thus preserving attributes that do not have the greatest reproductive potential. This diversity exists because *it has survival value for the species.* It gives each community a variety of talents to call on, each member contributing to the pool of skills of value to the community. It no longer is necessary for all to be good at the same thing; an individual can excel in one particular ability and share the fruits of his talents with those excelling in others. Interestingly, the other most highly social animals, the ants, have occupational specialists, suggesting the value of diversity. They also have achieved this by nongenetic means, using chemical substances on the larvae, not unlike that depicted by Aldous Huxley in his "utopian" *The Brave New World.* Without culture, natural selection works by favoring individuals in those activities that are most essential to the common lifestyle of the species, which makes polymorphism impossible except for sexual dimorphism (which is possible because obviously every population must include both sexes).

Every human community profits from a wide variety of talents. Even in societies in which all the members of any age and sex category spend most of their time at the same tasks, some have mastered specialties of one kind or another. One sees this everywhere, but I know of only one tribal society that has deliberately institutionalized diversity. This is the Iatmul of New Guinea, described by Gregory Bateson (1936), in which the success of each clan in ritual rivalry requires victory in both military and verbal combat; thus each clan must be able to field both jocks and eggheads.[1] The evolution of culture that we examined in the preceding chapter

---

1. Bateson describes the ceremony of Naven in detail and suggests that the two types fit into Kretschmer's categories of physiological types.

would not be possible without this specialized use of knowledge, and industrial society is entirely dependent upon it. Unlike Huxley, the eugenicists seem unaware of this necessity, seeming to think that populations made in their own image would be utopian.[2]

Diversity is a mixed blessing. Inasmuch as it has proved successful to our species, we can assume that the advantages outweigh the costs. Loyalty, a requisite to preserving harmony and engagement in sacrificial acts, is often instilled by evoking hostility and the distrust of others. Many languages see their name for themselves as meaning "the people" and ipso facto see others as something less. Such hostility is not limited to differences in ethnicity and language; the hostility between the Watusi and the Hutu of Burundi had its basis in class conflict, while the Sebei farmers and pastoralists, though much intermarried, were very disdainful of one another because of minor differences in customs and capabilities.

This source of social conflict with its inherent discriminations has made it taboo to discuss human differences in this era of political correctness. Yet people do vary, and some of this variation does lie in inherent capacities. Despite the sensitive nature of this subject, I must address it because it is essential to recognize that we are not all alike as physical creatures. First, I must dispel some fallacies that beset discussions of the subject. The first and most important is the erroneous assumption that intelligence, moral probity, or any other major human quality is correlated with cosmetic items such as skin color and hair texture that are criteria for "race." The recurrent efforts to make the connection are simply unscientific because they try to correlate qualities between such loosely defined taxons as "race" and "intelligence." The second fallacy is to confuse "difference" with "better/worse"; to be different is not

---

2. I was bemused by the performance of the two geneticists at a conference on the future of science back when genetic engineering was on the horizon. One was a lean, cerebral man with a big head and a narrow chest and the other a burley outdoorsman wearing a macho, bulky, hand-knit sweater. They were describing the future of humanity that would emerge with these new eugenic possibilities, each unconsciously but unmistakably described an image of himself.

to be worse. The third fallacy is considering concepts like character, talent, and intelligence as if each were a single, global, monolithic trait rather than a confluence of a host of specific qualities or abilities. We do not inherit artistic "genius," but we probably do inherit differences in such matters as color sensitivity, manual dexterity, spatial memory, hand–eye coordination, pitch, voice timbre, and so on, which, when properly combined and under the proper stimuli, create exceptional performances we call genius. I offered a model of how we should think of such matters when I discussed infant socialization. We do not inherit a "social instinct," but probably do inherit those sociophilic traits discussed in an earlier chapter that go into making a successful mother–child relationship. That is the way we should think about the inheritance of all talents. Diversity should have been taken for granted, for we are a species whose success was built upon adaptability. Instead, we seem to fear it. We should celebrate individual variability just as we are learning to appreciate ethnic diversity.

Rather than leaving this at generalities, we should examine specific ways in which this issue plays itself out. I will examine the issue of sexual preference, one of the most divisive in America today. Homosexual practices were illegal in many states and homosexuality was listed as a psychiatric disorder until 1987, when it was removed from the *Diagnostic and Statistical Manual* (DSM), the psychiatrists' guidebook. Psychoanalysts long tried to "cure" it. I became convinced about 50 years ago that homosexuality could not be treated as an illness and that it is not brought on by traumatic experiences. I had met the late psychologist Evelyn Hooker, who was then doing pioneering research leading us to see that homosexual preference is a natural variation in the stimuli for sexual arousal. She had taken Rorschachs from men who recognized their own homosexuality but did not participate in the "gay culture"[3] that most of the openly homosexual men then

---

3. At the time of her study, "gay" had reference to the patterns of behavior of openly homosexual men, centered around occupations that were thought to be limited to such men, like hairdressing and interior decoration. The term has been co-opted by the homosexual community and has lost its ethnographic tinge.

enjoyed. Her mentor, Rorschach specialist Bruno Klopfer, could read inkblots as if they were tarot cards to identify homosexual men—though he could not tell how he did it. Yet Klopfer could not identify Hooker's nongay homosexual subjects. The inkblots therefore had been showing the *cultural traits* of the homosexual community rather than the *psychological* attributes of homosexual men. The protocols that Hooker shared with me gave no hint of any situational factors that could account for sexual preference, and I have long been convinced that homosexuality is biologically based—though not necessarily genetic. From an evolutionary point of view, once you have the mechanisms for group-oriented life, keeping nonreproductive people alive makes survival sense, as some students of primates have argued with respect to "maiden aunt" and grandmother monkeys.

Gender identification is a closely related but separate matter. Some people have so compulsive a sense of belonging to the sex opposite to the one that their genitals indicate that they make great social, psychological, and financial sacrifices to undergo surgical operations that will fit their genitals to their psychological gender identity. No one has so much as suggested that these attitudes are the result of social influences. It is compelling evidence that there is *a biological determinant for sexual identification* at work among these men and women. We inherit or otherwise acquire a biologically ingrained, stubborn sentiment involving our gender feelings. This conclusion, based on publicly known instances of gender-alteration cases, is supported by a recent study of 16 male neonates who had been born with what was identified as "cloacal exstrophy with severe phallic inadequacy" (in layman's terms, malformation in the anal area and unformed penis), 14 of whom had undergone an operation creating vaginas and were reassigned to the female sex at birth (the parents of the other two refused reassignment). All 16 engaged in more male-oriented behavior and attitudes in tests, and 8 of the 14 subjects declared themselves to be male, as did the 2 not reassigned. The data dramatically confirm the assumption that there is a significant inheritance factor in shaping the psychological outlook of boys and girls but enough diversity among the subjects of the study to suggest that there is some degree of flexibility (Reiner and Gearhart 2004).

The anomalous instances and the strong male identification of these cases of apparently mistaken sexual re-identification make it difficult to deny that the rest of us have inherent gender-oriented sentiments that have not been culturally acquired. (The study, incidentally, makes mockery of the efforts to get boys to play with dolls and give trucks to girls, which for a time was urged by some who assumed these to be culturally influenced attitudes.)

We understand no more about the role of genetics in determining human behavior now than we did at the beginning of the century of the gene. We do know, however, that the genetic transmission of information is subject to a kind of editing that shapes it to local needs. It is quite clear that we will not find the bodily representation of the soul in our genes; indeed, if it is to be located anywhere, the most likely place to find it is in the prefrontal lobes of the brain, though I'm dismayed by its negativity (see Sidebar 15).

Soul

When a wolf pup avoids meat that its dam refuses because she was once nauseated by the smell, it is responding to "borrowed experience" learned from its mother. When a chimpanzee youngster imitates its mother fishing for termites, it, too, is acting on acquired experience, presumably having aped the mother's firing patterns with its mirror neurons. This is the fundamental physical event that lies at the basis of culture, but it is not culture. Each of these experiences is a unique event and cannot be transposed into some other kind of activity; it came directly from one animal to another and was not mediated by a symbol system—by language. It is not a cultural act; it is not a symbolic act; it is merely learned behavior. There is no soul expressed in this, no symbolic presence.

Soul is a theological concept in Western thought, and all religions assume that there is some kind of transcendental existence for the spiritual aspect of human beings. It is the task of the scientist to see the secular side of belief, as Galileo and Darwin did regarding the heavens and the origin of humans. Souls do not obey the laws of thermodynamics, being the product of human belief, and so we need not look for logic and reason in their actions.

ARE THE PREFRONTAL LOBES THE SEAT OF THE SOUL?

From the neuroscientific point of view, ironically perhaps, the essence of "free will" appears to be the capacity for *inhibition*- the capacity to choose *not* to do something. What distinguishes human beings more than anything else from their nearest primate relatives is the development of a higher-level "self" system, which is organized fundamentally on *inhibitory* mechanisms. These mechanisms, which have their physical locus in the prefrontal lobes (the crowning glory of the human brain), bestow on us the capacity to *suppress* the primitive, stereotyped compulsions that are encoded in our inherited and emotional memory systems. On this basis, in inhibitory prefrontal lobes may be regarded, with some justification, as the very tissue of our humanity.

The prefrontal lobes mature after birth, mainly in two massive spurts around the ages of 2 and 5 years, but they continue to develop throughout the first two decades of life. They are therefore heavily "experience-dependant." The experiences that shape the activity of these executive mechanisms in the earliest years of life will determine their individual structure. The application of their inherent (neurochemical) inhibitory capacities is, accordingly, literally *sculpted* by the parental (and other authority) figures who guide this aspect of the child's development during the critical early years. This "sculpting" process appears to be governed by at least two things: first, by what parents *do*; second, by what they *say*.

Sohms and Turnbull 2000:281–282.

People everywhere have names, each person with his own. They may be taboo, they may be changed, but individuals everywhere are named. This recognizes the individuality of each person. Similarly, I know of no people in the world who fail to have some notion of the human soul. This recognizes that each individual also exists in the symbolic world. As with all things cultural, the specifics vary widely; there may be one or many souls, they may stay around to haunt the living or go elsewhere; they may demand placation or be expected to be of help; and so on. Shamans have souls that travel through space; sometimes the soul of a patient wanders from the body and the shaman must go and retrieve it. Animals and even inanimate things may be thought to have souls. The Aranda have souls that dwell in the "Dream Time," inhabiting the sacred churingas from the time they die and live in that other world until they return to earth by entering a woman's womb. The Tlingit believe that the soul of a brave warrior who fell in battle defending his clan or a woman who dies in giving birth to a child will go to the "highest heaven." The Sebei fear the dead and put corpses out for the hyenas so the soul cannot find its way back; they nevertheless honor dead ancestors by pouring libations at the entry to the cattle kraal for those they respect but out in the bush for those they fear and despise. If we want to understand the dead soul's behavior, we must look at the living—at the tensions and yearnings suffusing the society, for souls are a projection of collective feeling. They are an expression of and an influence on what the Germans call the *Zeitgeist*, the spirit of the time. The Aranda sense of the unity and continuity of the clan places every person in a universal and eternal social entity, with all the accumulated sentiments that time has bestowed on it; the Tlingit is reinforcing the strength of the clan in a society in which the clan defines status and privilege. The Sebei treat the dead with the same manipulative behavior that they treat one another in life—they use the friendly ones and avoid the others.

Philosophy has long been rationalizing the soul—that is, bringing it into the domain of logical thought. In Western philosophy that task began with Aristotle. Jonathan Lear summarizes Aristotle's view: "Soul is not a special ingredient which breathes life into a lifeless body; it is a certain aspect of a living organism" (1988:97). He goes on to say that Aristotle distinguishes humanity in having the ability to understand, in his sense of inquiry. Lear explains: "Understanding . . . is man's capacity to grasp how things really are, not just how they immediately present themselves. And as man does come to understand the world, he comes to understand something fundamental about himself; namely, that understanding the world lies at the bottom of what he is" (117). This capacity to construct a world of reality was already seen by Aristotle to be the essence of being human. Anthropologists, who have looked at the diverse understandings that humans have propounded over the years, may attribute this claim of understanding what the world is *really* like as being philosophers' hubris and say that it should read that it is the essence of humans to *try to understand* the world in some terms. And then, given the self-fulfilling prophesy, the world *becomes* as they know it.

Some 19th and 20th-century writers' observations on human nature were summarized by Richard Schacht (1990) in an essay urging the importation of European "philosophical anthropology" to the United States. He concludes a discussion of Marx, Kierkegaard, and Nietzsche by noting that, despite their manifest differences, these men share "the idea [that] while actual human beings may come to have natures which are in various ways determinate, this determinateness is something they *acquire* in one way or another in the course of their lives, rather than something with which they are *commonly endowed* by virtue of their being instances of the human kind of entity" (161, Schacht's italics). Being philosophers, they do not say what the "how" is, but they are anticipating the behavioral scientist's view of the soul as a thing-in-process.

With the extension of scientific investigation into the nature of humans, it was inevitable that scholars would examine the secular side of the soul. Pioneering American psychologist William James saw this quintessential human quality as the self or, rather, the several selves. James (1950) tries to identify and name the several aspects of the self as distinct entities and sees the social self as "other-dependant," noting that each person has as many selves as he is involved with groups of people whose opinions he cares about. These ideas have been the basis for research in social psychology by both sociologists and psychologists, evoking concepts like persona, self, ego, status, and role in order to see the individual in terms of his relation to others.

Freud famously split the human psyche into three entities that he labeled id, ego, and superego (actually, he used ordinary German words rather than Latin ones, *es, ich,* and *überich*) to separate out what might roughly be identified as our innate drives, our sense of self, and our conscience. These homunculi—the id, ego, and superego—seem as quaint now as do the demons of an earlier time. They are, of course, merely reification of the *processes* they represent, probably influenced by Plato's tripartite souls: language and reason, bodily appetites and needs, and emotional drives

(Lavine 1984). As a therapist seeking cures for people with psychological and emotional problems, Freud focused on the personal experiences his patients had with family members and not the social environment in which they were embedded. He used other cultures only in efforts to elucidate psychological universals: human nature, not human variability. The anthropologists whose work we saw earlier and who had taken their inspiration from Freud were trying to bring these dynamics into cross-cultural research to show that cultural sentiments are at work in shaping attitudes.

The Soul and Culture

A. I. Hallowell (1967) brought the Freudian-inspired self into anthropological discourse. Hallowell was part of the early psychological anthropology movement. His work with the Ojibwa, using Rorschach and other personality tests, showed that the Ojibwa individual's understanding of reality was all of a piece with his fantasy life and that these in turn were personalized extensions of the mythic world that they had internalized from the stories, prayers, and rituals of their past. "Self awareness in man," Hallowell wrote, "cannot be taken as an isolated psychological phenomena [sic], however, if we are to understand the full range and depth of its human significance. For it is becoming increasingly apparent that this peculiar human phenomena is the focus of complex, and functionally dependent, sets of linguistic and cultural variables that enter into the personal adjustment of human beings as members of particular societies" (75). Later he says that we should "speak of the environment in which man lives as a 'culturally constructed behavioral environment'" (87).

This self, the secularized version of the human soul, is the product of the revolution that is revisited in every nursery in the history of the species. It is not a static thing, not really a thing as much as an emanation that is always a work in progress—not even finished after death, as it remains in the hearts and minds of those that it has influenced throughout life. The self gets its shape from the cumulative experience of its fellow human beings as these have been distilled by those who are responsible for the child's development. The perception that we humans take our shape from our experience of others is to me an ennobling view of humanity; I have no trouble seeing it as the soul, for it lessens the distance between the self and the other; it reaffirms that unity among all living things that I noted at the outset and that I find so gratifying and infuses it into the world of human interaction. It is a secular version of what is expressed in all religions, from ancient totemism to the sermons and homilies of every modern belief system.

The evidence that the cultural self can affect the biological being, that it literally changes that being's mind and brain, means that we as individuals have quite literally incorporated others within the physical parameters we think of as our selves. This transforms that phrase drawn from the behavioral sciences, "internalizing the other," from a metaphor into a description of actual physical events. This gives a new take on that ancient opposition between self and other. It is structured into the human condition, the self that devours the selfish gene. This suggests that the soul is not as immaterial as we think. When we say that our souls will continue in the minds and hearts of those we have touched in our lifetime, this is not just a figure of speech, but a physical reality, for we have helped to shape their brains as well as their minds. This raises an intriguing issue with respect to human cloning. It may be that Dolly was a perfect replica of her source, but this cannot be said about any human clone. No human adult is merely a product of his DNA; his very being has been transformed by his life experiences.

Recognizing this otherness in ourselves also gives us pause to think about what selfishness means. Our culture puts so much emphasis on individual accomplishment that we often disregard the fact that no accomplishment is ever an individual achievement as well as the fact that we would get little gratification if we did not have others to appreciate what we have done. And while we are on this trope of seeing the other in ourselves, we should pause over the notion of "altruism." I have not used that word in this book until now. Altruism is supposed to be a sacrificial act, but if helping another at some cost gives satisfaction to the doer, it is no longer purely sacrificial. As the economists would say, there is no cost–benefit loss. Some might feel that this denies the credit for such socially valued behavior, but it does not. It transfers the accolade from the act to the character of the person as one who adheres to social values.

Affect hunger—that innate but unheralded attribute at the core of this book—is a motivating force in each one of us and was a major force in shaping human history, taking over from biology the task of evolution. It has given each human being the urge to be part of some larger social whole and to be someone of consequence in it. This need for the other gives the cohesion that makes the unity of the social order possible. It has also spurred us in that competition for the recognition (and also, admittedly, for mates) that underlies the pursuit of excellence, which, over the millennia, has moved humanity from small bands of foragers toward an ever-accelerating evolutionary growth into becoming the creators of great art, architecture, literature, and music and not just to reach out to the heavens, but actually to invade them—all in but some 7,500 generations since the species appeared and merely 2,000 since the Upper Paleolithic began. *Ad astra per aspera*, indeed!

There is perhaps no better way to evaluate the quality of a culture than to learn how the people gratify their affect hunger and the degree to which the society enables them to do so. There is no better measure of a person than to learn how he seeks to gratify, or wants to be able to gratify, his hunger for affect.

We have not appreciated this. We have been derisive of it for creating the desire for brownie points and chasing the fragile and ever-changing symbols of social standing; we have failed to realize that the urge for mother love has led us to aspire to be proper members of our community and to take on its duties and responsibilities when our turn comes. Freud has led us to confuse our desire for maternal comforts with our ancient urges to couple with the opposite sex, condemning that urge with responsibility for our wanting to commit vile and contemptible "Oedipal" crimes, when it is really the crucial urge that takes us outside the realm of mere biological beings and into a whole new mode of existence. It is the nurturant love, and the affect hunger that energizes it, that induces us to live in concert with others, to collaborate in creating and maintaining social order, and to inspire us to a creativity that has constantly raised our sights to build ever more elaborate edifices—social and physical. The very hubris that has led us to these creative heights seems also to let us overlook our dependency on them and thus, with tragic irony, may ultimately be our undoing.

9

A View of the Bridge

Ullica Segerstråle (2000) concludes her sociological examination of the intellectual contest between cultural understanding on one side and sociobiology and evolutionary psychology on the other, with a chapter entitled, "The Battle for the Soul—and for the Soul of Science." In her introductory chapter, she anticipates the drama she is to disclose in the book by picturing it as opera. Truth and Clarity are to emerge from the fog enveloping the stage as the opera ends but, perhaps unwilling to disclose the bodies lying all over, she notes that the drama is not ended and says that these noble spirits are yet to appear. I also see the quarrels of anthropology over the nature versus nurture issue as a bloody, overblown drama with enormously appealing plot threads that reach into the psyche, playing on our deepest prejudices and predilections with their theological and philosophical undertones. Our heroine—Affect Hunger—comes onto this scene as go-between, moving the plot forward to the point where nature and nurture recognized their mutual interdependence.

Duality

The drama that is at issue is at the base of a much-examined and fundamental duality that came into being with the emergence of humanity. It is the conflict between two sets of directives, the ancient one carrying the banner that proclaims its individuality and argues for its inalienable rights, girded with the fighting spirit and its sexual prowess; the younger one urging the desires for unity and communion. These two spirits thread throughout history and have been expressed in many idioms: They are the yin and yang of ancient Chinese wisdom and the feminine and masculine principles in much of Western thought.

This duality can easily segue into male versus female and even good versus bad, but that is the wrong way to go. To be sure, women are more deeply involved with affective roles than are men, as their role of motherhood demands, and it is reasonable to assume—and a good deal of evidence shows—that they are better endowed with those traits that enable them to perform such roles than men are. Men also have continued in the more public, protective role that mammalian males so often perform and are endowed with physical and perhaps also behavioral characteristics to perform such roles. But this is not an either/or matter. One of the central themes of this book has been the high degree of flexibility that characterizes our species, and this applies to gender roles and capacities both in diversity among members of the same sex and flexibility in individual behavior.

Nor should this duality be seen as good versus evil, though it is easy to fall into the trap of seeing it so, for most of us face the dichotomy with deep-seated personal predilections, whether we are aware of them or not. We humans evolved with the capacity for violence and the desire for vengeance as well as the capacity for tenderness and caring because both were essential to the evolutionary process by which we came into being, not out of some kind of evolutionary mistake. No doubt that old egocentric urge for dominance and the capacity for violence had survival value at a time when our species was fighting its way into existence, but this urge is not just an atavistic remnant of some savage past. The duality between the fierce and the sweet is essential to our species; it is the cross we must bear for the privilege of being human. It is the work of culture to maintain the balance between them.

Affect Hunger

Affect hunger is rooted in biology and emerges with culture. It ties the two together. Affect hunger does not leave the realm of biology, for its very existence plays a role in survival, first by contributing to the development of the central nervous system and second by motivating us to entice the maternal care that is needed to live in a human world. Affect hunger thus brings the infant to culture by inducing it to attend to the lessons set forth on what the culture expects and what must be done to satisfy its demands. It is truly a bridge—a bridging concept that leaves both biology and culture intact.

You can see immediately why I do not call it *the* key but only the missing key to our understanding of that transformation to humanity. In the rest of this concluding chapter I want to summarize and highlight the focal points in the scenario that I have developed here, examining affect hunger in the context of the other factors that are involved in this transformation and have long been recognized. In doing this, I show how, as students of human behavior, we must look under the veil of our own culture to protect ourselves from the misleading language of normal discourse and associated customs, reexamining familiar words that have masked important differences or obscured vital similarities. At the close, I point to the considerations as to why this view of humanity is needed for an understanding of everyday problems.

Love

The most important element in this understanding is the decoupling of the two facets of love, which will enable us to appreciate the special role that nurturance plays in human existence. I am not alone in recognizing the role that infancy and early childhood play in human life. Whole professions are devoted to its study—studies from which I have drawn crucial information. The decoupling of nurturant from sexual love lets us look at the former without entangling ourselves in the drama of the latter. It also enables us to keep some of Freud's seminal insights regarding the dynamics of what he called the Oedipal complex. By treating the yearning for parental love, which is the very fount of cultural transmission, as being an expression of sexual fantasies and murderous intent, Freud condemned the most vital force in human behavior to the garbage pail of sexual aberration. We cannot understand affect hunger without recognizing the necessity of maternal affection, nor can we disregard the dynamics that it creates throughout life. It is a sad commentary that the only dynamic theory for the development of culture in the past century was based on the outlook of persons with manifest pathologies. The breach of the normal often leads to insight in the underlying dynamics, as every structural geologist and brain scientist will readily confirm, but it is what the earth's tremor or the brain trauma reveals that is the true discovery, not the shocks that brought them about. The pains of the men and women whose dramas Freud examined were real and his insights telling, but the theories he spun on them are not.

Language

We must appreciate the central role language plays in this revolution. We cannot disregard the unique quality of human speech that differentiates it from all other animal communication. Grammar and syntax serve to disengage what is being said in a speech act from what is going on in this place at this time among those present, enabling us to fabricate the diverse worlds in which people live. This ability must rest on a unique evolutionary development in the human brain, which is why we all have that big round box balanced on top of our spines. How it works remains a mystery, I know—but there it is. We get a glimmering of its working from the light being shed by the newly discovered mirror neurons and in the brain physiology of neuropeptides. We have long recognized the essential role language plays in the existence of culture, but here I want to emphasize that it was crucial to bringing culture onto the scene, for it is the translation of infants' experiences into the meanings of the world around them that differentiates maternal care among humans from the instruction other newborns get from their mothers. It is at the mother's bosom that the child acquires those radical new motivations that lead him to act in ways so contrary to his animal heritage. Other animal mothers teach their young how to hunt and kill and what food to avoid, but they are taught by demonstration, which, by definition, is in the here and now.

Fabrication

The close tie between language and making things, which I find logically compelling, solves a problem that has always been troubling, namely, providing a survival advantage for the formative stages of the complex business of human speech during the evolutionary process. Poor vision and poor hearing are better than none, but it is hard to see the embryonic forms of language offering enough gain to be advantageous in their own right. But if the mental processes required for language are the same as those used for making things, the issue is solved. A poor tool is better than none. We don't have to imagine the beginnings of making things, for the archaeological record, poor as it is, is both unequivocal and plausible in showing the gradual improvement of technical proficiency. In this co-evolutionary development, language may or may not have been helpful in making things; I think it was, but it may merely have hitched a free ride. The idea that these two most diagnostic features of humanity are closely linked in origin seems like a natural; the supporting evidence from the mirror neurons transforms this from conjecture to hypothesis.

Communicating Feeling

It is also important to disengage language from the vocalizations and gestures of our primate ancestry. These natural elements in our heritage are not used for explaining things but are always concerned with ongoing events that call for immediate responses. Anyone who thinks that language is a useful way to communicate feelings has never had a lovers' quarrel or been to a faculty meeting. When words are used to convey stress, they are epithets that take on the character of animal calls; their meaning, if any, has no relevance to matters at hand. When we try to convey our feelings to others, we embellish the cold formality of speech with such devices as metaphor, rhyme, cadence, onomatopoeia, and other poetic forms, if we have the literary talent; if not we substitute curses and vulgar epithets. Such embellishments help convey how we feel, but only the most skillful literary talent can get listeners actually to *feel* what he wants them to. We use the natural cries and gestures of everyday life to express hurt, fear, or love and put them together in rituals to raise such acts to the level of standardized communication—but not to the level of language.

For the purpose of general communication, humans have everywhere harnessed these natural forms of communication to performing rituals. Rituals are intended to communicate to those present, so the inherent limitations of animal cries are no drawback. Rituals harness the vocalizations and behavioral attributes that are inherently associated with feelings, both pleasurable and painful, both elating and depressing, to evoke the desired feelings among all those present. They are therefore, like language, a device for communicating, but they are for transmitting sentiment. Because they are using natural aspects of the human animal, they did not require a special evolutionary development. They are a product of culture.

Cultural Worlds

Though speech may have come to us in the beginning just as a means of sending messages, our species has everywhere and presumably always used it to create narratives, so people can share a picture of the world with those within its reach. Other animals may have a mental image of the immediate environment, but it can be shared only with those who are experiencing it together, and only to the extent that it has a physical presence. But all human children are walking into a preconstructed world deeper and deeper with every word they add to their vocabulary, until it fills out a more-or-less coherent picture of the universe that is more-or-less identical with the one held by their mentors. All the children enter such a world gradually as they are growing up, living in this constructed world long before they can actually have the physical experiences of that world.

The Symbolic Self

All human life is lived in such a created symbolic world and all the inhabitants of this world are also symbols, and so each person is a symbol to others and, without being aware of it, is a symbol to himself or herself. It is to that symbolic self that each person comes to devote his energies and talents, for it is that symbolic being that comes to be thought of as the *persona*. That desire for the stroking, holding, and feeding that was originally sought becomes redirected to the symbolic expression of acceptance and approval from an ever-widening presence of others. These are received in response to the quality of performance in the activities that are expected in accordance with his role in the community as defined by its rules and customs. They come in diverse forms, from smiles and nods to words of approval, to accolades, to ever more remote and impersonal expressions—to the extent that they may be fully dehumanized in such a mass society as our own. Those actions that had animal origins in order to protect self and progeny were redirected to serve the welfare and advancement of this symbolic self, this ego. These rewards can be gratifying, and their absence or negation can be traumatic blows to that ego.

The pursuit of this symbolic self can become so intense that it takes over all the time and energy to the neglect of those desires that was its original aim—that direct physical human warmth under which those urges were born. Symbolic rewards, however sweet, do not fulfill the physical yearning. We recognize this in many ways in our standard social discourse, as when a public figure resigns his post "in order to spend more time with his family" or the successful modern woman is torn between her rewarding career and her yearning for children. Under simpler conditions, the two sets of goals were not so mutually exclusive. The successful hunter bringing a buck into camp to share with family and others in the band will get expressions of appreciation along with a meal of venison and the vegetables his wife had collected. The husband and wife working the farm as a team are in constant interaction and share the rewards of their collaboration. One does not have to idealize the family as the only means of having close personal warmth. I have already noted that husband and wife among the Sebei have a hostile relationship, but the men have close bonds to their age mates while the women in the farming sector work in collaboration to cultivate their gardens.

We did not abandon our animal past but only tamed it, as best we could. With the growth of societies and the depersonalization of the workplace, the gratifications for the ego and the satisfactions of the body have increasingly drifted apart. Much of the energy that people devote to ego gratification also fills their larders, advances their health and physical well-being, and gets mates and progeny. But despite Chagnon's theories about the Yanomamo, this does not necessarily increase the progeny of those who are most successful in this contest, for, as has long been known, the best birth control method is increased prosperity—to make everybody middle class. Ironically, this inhibition of the selfish aim of "the selfish gene" turns out to have been a most successful gambit for species survival, as Homo sapiens multiplied. Giving the species wit at the expense of brute strength turned out to have been a good evolutionary gamble. If we had been watching over the five to ten million years of the transition, I doubt that many of us would have put our money on it—and some people still aren't convinced.

Affect Hunger and Cultural Evolution

Once all the elements were in place, the evolution of culture took off with great speed. This pace is a consequence of harnessing the urges to excel to the social aim of being the best (whatever "best" may mean in that culture) in the community. Some significant portion of that energy went into ways of improving practical matters in the food quest and other life-saving and life-enhancing innovations. The result is a palpable exponential cultural growth over the history of the species. This constant acceleration, which must have started with pre-*sapiens* hominids, has been clearly manifested since the Upper Paleolithic began and throughout history. It was repeated in the New World. It has a continuity that is independent of particular societies; in fact, the evolution of culture, like the evolution of life, seems to depend upon the shedding of the old. Be that as it may, the exponential curve is not mysterious, for the more the technology, the greater the possibilities for fruitful innovation; the more total the time that is freed from the food quest, the more time for seeking and finding further innovations. I call this the build-a-better-mousetrap cycle—the urge for status leads to an urge for creativity that leads to greater productive capacity that leads to more people with the urge for status advancement. All this iterated down the ages, accumulating knowledge as it goes.

There are downsides to this urge for mastery. The first is that it can carry individuals to such fascination with the process itself that they become like compulsive gamblers, so carried away with the mastery of one particular form of status reward—money, power, fame, or following—that they are never satisfied. This can be both socially destructive and self-destructive, best exemplified by the miser who cannot spend any money for enjoyment and dies with a large secret bank account. Nor is it just a modern phenomenon, but can occur wherever a surplus of material resources frees people from the daily pressures of living. The Northwest Coast potlatch is an example of the institutionalization of such excessive involvement with conspicuous waste. Similar, less formalized excesses are reported among Melanesian "big men," with their obsessive concern for power. The destructive potential of such compulsion in pursuit of power is well known to history in the form of Caesars, Napoleons, and Hitlers.

A more subtle negative effect of the intensive search for status is that it can lead to the neglect of the basic need that affect hunger was designed to seek—the physical expression of affection itself. I have devoted the last few chapters to the socialization of affect, which is what makes it interesting to the cultural anthropologist and important to the history of the species, but we must remember that it was originally and still remains a physiological urge that our physical being still needs. We neglect the need for direct physical contact and the personal expression of affect at a cost to our physical and psychological being. My favorite literary expression of this is Citizen Kane, who could never recapture the feelings symbolized by Rosebud, the sled given to him by his parents. We see it in such small things as the response to pets by the warehoused elderly and such tragic things as youths turning to gangs when they feel barred from access to the more socially accepted forms of status.

Self and Other

These are manifestations of the major source of the difficulties of human social life: *the relation of self to other.* Human society depends on individual human beings being motivated to act on their own and in their own interest, but at the same time its effectiveness depends on their commitment to the social order to which they belong. This issue is far more pervasive even than the relationship between the sexes, which gets so much more public attention. Every society needs people who are able and willing to act on their own but it also needs people who act in the interest of the whole. It is best when both ends are served by the same persons and ideally in the same activity. Institutions are needed that maximize both, but they are not easy to devise and maintain, especially in complex societies. Ecological conditions often place a premium on one or the other of these. The emphasis was placed on subordination of individual freedom among the Zuni because their need for solidarity was imperative under the environmental conditions of the Southwestern desert. It contrasts to the Plains Indian pattern, in which individuals publicly bragged about their exploits in an economy of hunters and warriors, who must show initiative and daring and who must often go out on their own. Much of the underlying tensions among the Sebei lay in the fact that institutions of socialization had been designed for the relatively independent action that the pastoral mode of life called for but were ill-suited to the crowded conditions that plantain farming creates.

The ecological condition that shaped the American culture was the frontier. Its dominant qualities were the absolute requisite for personal ability and energy, the need for personal independence of action, and the unlimited possibilities for material reward for those endowed with these virtues. These attitudes have been institutionalized in many ways, starting with the "pursuit of happiness" phrase in the Declaration of Independence and the "states rights" principle in the Constitution. The conflict between individuality and social cohesion polarizes our political parties. The confrontation is also in the rhetoric of the Cold War, though fascistic control in the communist countries had as little resemblance to the socialist ideals of Karl Marx as the political manipulations of the market have to do with Adam Smith. This confrontation is false; every social order must find a balance between the reasonable interests of the individual and the needs of the community. Both the social relationships and the individual's performance are involved in affect fulfillment, the social context giving meaning to the person's actions.

This is the inescapable duality of the human world: the physical world of animal motives and self-interest and the symbolic world of cultural values and other-interest. This duality is inescapable, for both sets of demands are internalized. We see it over and over in the laments in the novels of first-generation hyphenated-Americans, the pull of the ethnic home-oriented past against the glamour of "success" in the broader world for the educated children, whether East European, Italian, or (more recently) Chinese and Southeast Asians. It was the central theme of William Foote White's *Corner Boys,* a classic study of Italian immigrants; Amy Tan's *The Joy Luck Club*; the movie *My Big Fat Greek Wedding*; and I daresay hundreds more. Nor is it just American; it appears, for instance, in the novels of Nigerian Chinua Achebe, as well as in studies of "acculturation" from all over the world. As with the Cinderella story, the plot remains the same while the artifacts and other particulars vary.

Affect hunger has put the human species in a unique position in the history of life on this planet, giving us an extraordinary power to change the world to our own liking. Its benefits are not only in the material things but also in our capacity to see, to understand, and to share our understandings. Had this not taken place I would not be writing these lines nor would you be reading them. And none of us could have learned the remarkable things that the evolutionary process has produced, one of which is ourselves learning about them.

This evolutionary process is a series of adjustments to the original impetus (established early to use wit at the expense of strength in the competition for existence) to build on the commitment to group collaboration. It all came together as a package that led to humanity. Over the millennia our ancestors used this wit to take us to where we now are.

One Final Thought

Understanding how we got to be human turns out to be one with understanding what humans are fundamentally like—which is what we really most want to know. Thus it turns out that the bridge to humanity is also the bridge to understanding ourselves.

Coda

In the Preface I said that a proper understanding of the motivating forces of human behavior is essential to formulating healthy public policies and I had planned to conclude this book with a programmatic statement. But where to start? Affect hunger is so fundamental to human existence that it invades every aspect of our being, so there could be no end in where to look. It begins with problems in the care of infants, goes on to the traumas of adolescence, and ends with the loneliness that exacerbates the pains of old age. It has to do with the quality of justice and the availability of opportunity; it has to do with the relationships between men and women, between ethnic groups, between employers and their work force, and among nations. You name it.

So I gave that up.

Instead, I invite you to think about the ills you see in our society. Are they related to affect deprivation? If so, consider the cultural attitudes and public policies that might alleviate them.

Consider the difficulties in having a sense of belonging: the decline of family; residential discontinuity; loss of neighborhoods (so important to children); weakened identification with region, state, and city; the loss of church suppers and the oxymoron of televised "congregations"; the disappearance of lodges and local clubs.

Consider what Thorstein Veblen called "the instinct of workmanship," the gratification from acts of creation that artisans and workmen get, as well as artists, and how this has been lost to automation and robotics, and how this is invading the professions—as, for instance, physicians becoming "health care providers."

Consider the cradle of affective relationships—literally, the cradle. The home has lost its importance and its structure for a large proportion of the population. What percent of the population can be deprived of cultural indoctrination without destroying the culture itself?

As you consider these matters, be introspective: What have been the forces that shape your own measurement of self? What gratifies your affect hunger?

References Cited

Ainsworth, Mary D. Salter. *Infancy in Uganda; Infant Care and the Growth of Love*. Baltimore: Johns Hopkins Press, 1967.

American Anthropological, Association. "Resolution on 'the New Synthesis.'" *Anthropology Newsletter* 1976.

Angulo, Jaime de. *Indians in Overalls*. San Francisco: City Lights Books, 1990.

Baker, L. D. "A Model Approach for Studying Race: Provocative Theory, Sound Science, and Very Good History." *American Anthropologist* 106, no. 1 (2004): 168–172.

Bates, E., and F. Dick. "Language, Gesture, and the Developing Brain." *Developmental Psychobiology* 40, no. 3 (2002): 293–310.

Bateson, Gregory. *Naven, a Survey of the Problems Suggested by a Composite Picture of the Culture of a New Guinea Tribe Drawn from Three Points of View*. Cambridge: Cambridge University Press, 1936.

Bateson, Gregory, and Margaret Mead. *Balinese Character, a Photographic Analysis*. New York: The New York Academy of Sciences, 1942.

Benedict, Ruth. *Patterns of Culture*. Boston: Houghton Mifflin, 1934.

Bowlby, John. *Attachment*. New York: Basic Books, 1982. Reprint.

Chagnon, Napoleon A. *Yanomamö: The Fierce People*. 3rd ed. New York: Holt, Rinehart and Winston, 1983.

———. "Life Histories, Blood Revenge, and Warfare in a Tribal Population." *Science* 239, no. 4843 (1988): 985–992.

Cockburn, Alexander. "What Happens When Genocide Poses as Science." *Los Angeles Times*, October 8, 2000, p. 5.

Darwin, Charles. *The Expression of the Emotions in Man and Animals*. London: J. Murray, 1872.

Dawkins, Richard. *The Selfish Gene*. New ed. Oxford: New York, 1989.

Dennell, R. "The World's Oldest Spears." *Nature* 385, no. 6619 (1997): 767–768.

Edgerton, Robert B. *The Individual in Cultural Adaptation; a Study of Four East African Peoples*. Berkeley: University of California Press, 1971.

Erikson, Erik H. *Observations on the Yurok: Childhood and World Image*. Berkeley: University of California Press, 1943.

Falk, Dean. *Primate Diversity*. New York: W. W. Norton & Co., 2000.

Feldman, R., and C. W. Greenbaum. "Affect Regulation and Synchrony in Mother–Infant Play as Precursors to the Development of Symbolic Competence." *Infant Mental Health Journal* 18 (1997): 4–23.

Fleck, Ludwik. *Genesis and Development of a Scientific Fact*. Chicago: University of Chicago Press, 1979.

Freeman, Derek. *Margaret Mead and Samoa: The Making and Unmaking of an Anthropological Myth*. Cambridge, Mass.: Harvard University Press, 1983.

Freud, Sigmund. *Totem and Taboo*. New York: Random House, 1909.

Gallese, V. "From Grasping to Language: Mirror Neurons and the Origin of Social Communication." In *Towards a Science of Consciousness* 3 ed. D. J. Chalmers. Boston: The MIT Press, 1999.

Geschwind, N. "Specializations of the Human-Brain." *Scientific American* 241, no. 3 (1979): 180–199.

Gibbs, W. W. "The Unseen Genome: Beyond DNA." *Scientific American* 289, no. 6 (2003): 106–113.

Goldschmidt, Walter. "Social Organization in Native California and the Origin of Clans." *American Anthropologist* 50, no. 3 (1948): 444–456.

———. "Ethics and the Structure of Society." *American Anthropologist*, no. 53 (1951): 506–524.

———. *Man's Way; a Preface to the Understanding of Human Society*. New York: Holt, 1959.

———. *Comparative Functionalism: An Essay in Anthropological Theory*. Barkeley: University of California Press, 1966.

———. *Kambuya's Cattle; the Legacy of an African Herdsman*. Berkeley: University of California Press, 1969.

———. "The Economics of Brideprice Among the Sebei and in East Africa." *Ethnology* 13, no. 4 (1972): 311–331.

———. *Culture and Behavior of the Sebei: A Study in Continuity and Adaptation*. Berkeley: University of California Press, 1976.

———. *The Sebei: A Study in Adaptation*. New York: Holt, Rinehart and Winston, 1986.

———. *The Human Career: The Self in the Symbolic World*. Cambridge: Blackwell, 1990.

———. *The Valley of the Clones*. Los Angeles, n.d.

Goldschmidt, Walter Rochs, and Harold Edson Driver. *The Hupa White Deerskin Dance*. Berkeley: University of California Press, 1940.

Hallowell, A. Irving. *Culture and Experience*. New York: Schocken Books, 1967.

Harlow, Harry Frederick. *Love in Infant Monkeys*. San Francisco: W. H. Freeman, 1959.

Harlow, Harry Frederick, and Clara Mears Harlow, ed. *From Learning to Love: The Selected Papers of Harry F. Harlow*. New York: Praeger, 1986.

Hauser, M. D., N. Chomsky, and W. T. Fitch. "The Faculty of Language: What Is It, Who Has It, and How Did It Evolve?" *Science* 298, no. 5598 (2002): 1569–1579.

Herrnstein, Richard J., and Charles A. Murray. *The Bell Curve: Intelligence and Class Structure in American Life*. New York: Free Press, 1994.

Hrdy, Sarah. *Mother Nature: A History of Mothers, Infants, and Natural Selection*. New York: Pantheon Books, 1999.

Iacoboni, M., R. P. Woods, M. Brass, H. Bekkering, J. C. Mazziotta, and G. Rizzolatti. "Cortical Mechanisms of Human Imitation." *Science* 286, no. 5449 (1999): 2526–2528.

Insel, T., and L. Young. "The Neurobiology of Attachment." *Nature Reviews Neuroscience* 2 (2001): 129–136.

James, William. *The Principles of Psychology*. Authorized unabridged ed. New York: Dover Publications, 1950.

Johnson, M. H., S. Dziurawiec, H. Ellis, and J. Morton. "Newborns' Preferential Tracking of Face-Like Stimuli and Its Subsequent Decline." *Cognition* 40, no. 1–2 (1991): 1–19.

Kilbride, J., and P. Kilbride. "Sociocultural Factors and the Early Manifestation of Sociability Behavior Among Baganda Infants." *Ethos* 2 (1974): 296–314.

Kilbride, P., M. Robbins, and J. Kilbride. "The Comparative Motor Development of Baganda, American White, and American Black Infants." *American Anthropologist*, no. 72 (1970): 1422–1428.

Kummer, Hans. *Primate Societies; Group Techniques of Ecological Adaptation*. Chicago: Aldine Atherton, 1971.

Lavine, T. Z. *From Socrates to Sartre: The Philosophic Quest*. New York: Bantam Books, 1984.

Lear, Jonathan. *Aristotle: The Desire to Understand*. New York: Cambridge University Press, 1988.

Maine, Henry Sumner Sir. *Ancient Law; Its Connection with the Early History of Society and Its Relation to Modern Ideas*. Boston: Beacon Press, 1963.

Maslow, Abraham H. *Toward a Psychology of Being*. 2nd ed. Princeton, N.J.: Van Nostrand, 1968.

McInerney, J., and M. Rothstein. *Behavioral Genetics*. U.S. Dept. of Energy, Human Genome Project, September 17, 2004. www.ornl.gov/sci/techresources/Human_Genome/elsi/behavior.shtml. Accessed October 24, 2004.

Mead, Margaret. *Coming of Age in Samoa; a Psychological Study of Primitive Youth for Western Civilization*. New York: Morrow, 1961.

Meltzoff, A. N., and M. K. Moore. "Imitation of Facial and Manual Gestures by Human Neonates." *Science* 198, no. 4312 (1977): 75–78.

Miller, Stephen G. *Arete: Greek Sports from Ancient Sources*. Berkely: University of California Press, 2004.

Nowak, Ronald M., and John L. Paradiso, eds. *Walker's Mammals of the World*. 4th ed. Baltimore: John Hopkins University Press, 1983.

Papousek, Hanus, and Mechthild Papousek. "Early Ontogeny of Human Social Interaction: Its Biological Roots and Social Dimensions." In *Human Ethology: Claims and Limits of a New Discipline*, ed. Mario von Corp. New York: Cambridge University Press, 1979.

Pinker, Steven. *The Language Instinct*. New York: W. Morrow and Co., 1994.

Ramachandran, V. S. *Mirror Neurons and Imitation Learning as the Driving Force Behind "the Great Leap Forward" in Human Evolution*. www.edge.org. Accessed October 17, 2002.

Reiner, W. G., and J. P. Gearhart. "Discordant Sexual Identity in Some Genetic Males with Cloacal Exstrophy Assigned to Female Sex at Birth." *New England Journal of Medicine* 350, no. 4 (2004): 333–341.

Rizzolatti, G., and M. A. Arbib. "Language Within Our Grasp." *Trends in Neurosciences* 21, no. 5 (1998): 188–194.

Rushton, J. Philippe. *Race, Evolution, and Behavior: A Life History Perspective.* New Brunswick, N.J.: Transaction Publishers, 1995.

Sapir, Edward. The status of linguistics as a science. *Language* 5 (1929): 207–214.

Schacht, R. "Philosophical Anthropology—What, Why and How." *Philosophy and Phenomenological Research* 50 (1990): 155–176.

Segerstråle, Ullica Christina Olofsdotter. *Defenders of the Truth: The Battle for Science in the Sociobiology Debate and Beyond.* Oxford: New York, 2000.

Shulevitz, J. "Academic Warfare." *New York Times Book Review*, Feb. 11, 2001, p. 35.

Siegel, D. J. "Toward an Interpersonal Neurobiology of the Developing Mind: Attachment Relationships, 'Mindsight,' and Neural Integration." *Infant Mental Health Journal* 22, no. 1–2 (2001): 67–94.

Snow, C. P. *The Two Cultures and the Scientific Revolution.* New York: Cambridge University Press, 1959.

Solms, M., and E. Nersessian. "Freud's Theory of Affect: Questions for Neuroscience." *Neuro-psychoanalysis* 1, no. 1 (1999): 5–14.

Solms, M., and O. Turnbull. *The Brain and the Inner World: An Introduction to the Neuroscience of Subjective Experience.* New York: Other Press, 2002.

Spencer, Baldwin Sir, and Francis James Gillen. *The Arunta: A Study of a Stone Age People.* London: Macmillan, 1927.

Spitz, René A. *The First Year of Life; a Psychoanalytic Study of Normal and Deviant Development of Object Relations.* New York: International Universities Press, 1965.

Stein, L. D. "Human Genome—End of the Beginning." *Nature* 431, no. 7011 (2004): 915–916.

Thieme, H. "Lower Palaeolithic Hunting Spears from Germany." *Nature* 385, no. 6619 (1997): 807–810.

Tierney, Patrick. "The Fierce Anthropologist." *The New Yorker*, October 9, 2000, pp. 50–61.

———. *Darkness in El Dorado: How Scientists and Journalists Devastated the Amazon.* Paperback ed. New York: Norton, 2001.

Tobias, P. V. "Twenty Questions About Human Evolution." *Human Evolution International Journal of Anthropology, and Global Bioethics* (2003): 9–64.

Trevarthen, Colwyn. "Instincts for Human Understanding and for Cultural Cooperation: Their Development in Infancy." In *Human Ethology: Claims and Limits of a New Discipline*, ed. Mario von Cranach. New York: Cambridge University Press, 1979.

Turnbull, Colin M. *The Forest People*. New York: Simon and Schuster, 1961.

———. *The Mbuti Pygmies: An Ethnographic Survey*. New York: American Museum of Natural History, 1965.

———. *The Mbuti Pygmies: Change and Adaptation*. New York: Holt Rinehart and Winston, 1983.

Veblen, Thorstein. *The Theory of the Leisure Class; an Economic Study of Institutions*. New York: The Macmillan Company, 1899.

Waldrop, M. Mitchell. *Complexity: The Emerging Science at the Edge of Order and Chaos*. New York: Simon & Schuster, 1992.

Weber, Max. *The Protestant Ethic and the Spirit of Capitalism*. Student's ed. New York: Scribner, 1958.

Weisner, T. "Why Ethnography Should Be the Most Important Method in the Study of Human Development." In *Ethnography and Human Development: Context and Meaning in Social Inquiry*, ed. R. Shweder. Chicago: University of Chicago Press, 1996.

Westen, D. "Towards a Clinically and Empirically Sound Theory of Motivation." *International Journal of Psycho-Analysis* 78 (1997): 521–548.

Wilson, Edward O. *Sociobiology: The New Synthesis*. Cambridge, Mass.: Belknap Press of Harvard University Press, 1975.

Winans, E. V. *Shambala: The Constitution of a Traditional State*. Berkeley: University of California Press, 1962.

Wynn, T. "Intelligence of Later Acheulean Hominids." *Man* 14, no. 3 (1979): 371–391.

Yovsi, R. D., and H. Keller. "Breastfeeding: An Adaptive Process." *Ethos* 31, no. 2 (2003): 147–171.

Zalewski, D. "Anthropology Enters the Age of Cannibalism." *New York Times*, October 8, 2000, Sec. 4.

Index